How To Be A Christian
Og Keep

Rock and Fire Press
Salinas, CA

How To Be A Christian
© 2019 by Og Keep

All Rights Reserved.
No portion of this work may be reproduced in any form or by any means without the prior written permission of the author, except for brief excerpts in reviews and criticism.

Cover Photos © 2019 by Og Keep
All Rights Reserved.

Library of Congress Catalog Number:

**ISBN-13:
978-1-949005-00-4 (Print)
978-1-949005-01-1 (eBook)**

FIRST EDITION
First Printing

Rock and Fire Press
Salinas, CA

Acknowledgements

Many individuals contributed information, or wisdom, or both, to the writing of this book. There may still be errors herein, of fact, logic, or style, despite the best efforts of those listed below.
For those errors, the author is solely responsible.

The author gratefully acknowledges and thanks:

Cam, Randy, Utah, Tall, and the entire forum
for their ongoing encouragement, and the Lulu crew:
Maggie, Rick, Jean-Paul, Ron, Kevin, Paul, Seamus et al.,
for advice, discussions, support, and general help.
In addition, sermons of, and personal discussions with,
Chase A. Thompson have proven invaluable
in helping to refine some of the points herein.

To all of the above:
I could not have done this without you.

Thank you.

"Quite often a man goes on for years imagining that the religious teaching that had been imparted to him since childhood is still intact, while all the time there is not a trace of it left in him."

-Leo Tolstoy, *Confession, pt. 1, ch. 1.*

STAGE ZERO
Finding the Faith

OKAY, SO MAYBE you suddenly realized that you were raised as a "Christian" but you have no idea what that really means. Or maybe you went to Sunday School and have a vague mental picture of God and Jesus and a boatload of animals. Oh, and a couple of naked people in a garden with an apple and a snake.

Maybe you managed to live your entire life so far without ever going into a church or being around a church. Maybe you were raised in a different faith, or no faith at all, or with a strong distaste for the Christian faith.

Whatever the reason, you have opened a book to find out more about Christianity. This will be a simple book, starting at the ground level, and it will progress into a complex book, giving you a deeper insight into the Christian faith. It will not be an over-your-head book about the Defenestration of Prague and the Diet of Worms (neither of which is as gross as it sounds). It will be a book that will meet you where you are and encourage you to the next level.

Christianity is a very simple faith, from the Stage 0 level. It teaches that mankind is inherently flawed, and that God, rather than expecting people to fix themselves so they could reach him, instead came down to their level to fix them. It teaches that the things humans do to themselves, to others, and to the world around them was resolved by the sacrifice of Jesus Christ on a cross.

And that's the simplest explanation of Christianity.

Of course, Christianity can also be very complex. People have debated details of Christianity for two thousand years, from whether Gentiles can become Christians (they can) to whether believers are still flawed (they are) and whether people are saved by their own choice or by God's choice (both).

As we move into the later stages of the book, we'll get to those points also. But for now, let's take Christianity at the ground level. In particular, let's look at the central teachings of Christianity, which are sometimes called the pre-Pauline gospel. Paul tells us what Peter and James taught him:

1. That Jesus of Nazareth died for the sins of mankind, and
2. Was buried, and
3. Rose from the dead on the third day, and
4. Was seen by many witnesses, and
5. Will return on the last day.

That's not a very complicated teaching. In fact, it's a very simple teaching. It is the central core of Christianity. When people in the book of Acts talk about sharing the gospel, these five points are what they mean. When Paul shared the gospel in the synagogues of Asia Minor, and later into Macedonia and Greece, this is the gospel that he shared. When people who are mentioned in the New Testament believed on Jesus Christ, these five points are what they believed.

As I say this, some of you might be thinking that these five points don't seem very believable. In fact, one or two of you might have bought this book in order to try to prove to your Christian friends that Christianity is false. In that case, your task is very simple. All you need to do is to find the bones of Jesus Christ.

Yes, that's right. Prove that Jesus of Nazareth did not rise from the dead – and his bones would do that very effectively – and you will demolish 2000 years of Christian teachings. If that's your goal, then off you go...

You're still here.

Well, maybe it's not quite that simple to disprove Christianity... After all, it's hard to find something that isn't there.

So let's go on. Maybe you'll have better luck as we look at it a bit more in depth.

The Apostle Paul, who wrote about half of the New Testament – possibly a bit more than half – wrote a good bit about how to be a Christian, and some people have gone so far as to make a "Roman Road" from his letter to the Romans. Paul taught this about becoming a Christian:

> 1. You've done bad things.
> *"There is none righteous, no, not one."* – Romans 3:10
> *"For all have sinned, and fall short of the Glory of God"*
> – Romans 3:23
>
> 2. That's a very big problem.
> *"For the wages of sin is death, but the gift of God is eternal life through Jesus Christ our Lord."* – Romans 6:23
>
> 3. But God loves you anyway.
> *"But God demonstrates His love thus: While we were still sinners, Christ died for us."* – Romans 5:8
>
> 4. And your bad deeds can be forgiven:
> *"If you confess with your mouth Jesus as Lord, and believe in your heart that God has raised Him from the dead, you shall be saved."* – Romans 10:9

It's pretty well indisputable that you've done bad things. You could argue that the things you've done aren't really wrong, or that there's no real scale for right and wrong anyway, and you can justify everything to yourself, so what's the big deal? But of course, we know that these are rationalizations. You're just telling yourself not to feel bad about things you've done, even though you know that you've hurt other people and even yourself.

If you're not willing to believe that you've ever done anything that hurt someone else, then you might wish to rethink your basic worldview. Throughout all of history, people have held the view that some things were morally right and others morally wrong. The entire concept of justice hinges upon this belief.

On the other hand, if you are willing to confess that you may be imperfect, and even (gasp!) inherently flawed, then we see a big problem when it comes to the teachings of Christianity. Sin leads to death. Note that Paul used the word "wages." Wages are not a punishment; they are a natural result of our actions. We work to gain a paycheck; the paycheck comes as a result of our work. It is something we have earned, something we deserve, and something that the laws of the state make utterly inevitable when the payday comes.

If we consider sin as a wage, we will see the relationship between sin and death: As we sin against, say, our friends – cheating them, lying to them, using them unjustly – we cause the death of our friendships. As we sin against a spouse, we see the death of the marriage and the death of our family. As we sin against a neighbor, we see the death of trust and community. As we sin against ourselves with alcohol or drugs, we see the deaths of our souls – the death of our consciences, of our reason, and even of our bodies. Sin against God – and all sin is really against God – causes the death of our relationship with God.

Sin leads to death: Physical and Spiritual death. It is as clear as daylight, as obvious as the sun in the sky.

But the gift of God – note that it is distinct from wages. A gift cannot be earned. It is not deserved. It is not the natural result of what we have done. It is not inevitable. We cannot work to gain God's favor, and this teaching is unique to Christianity. We are not expected to earn our way: God gives it to us as a gift.

Every true gift is given out of love. In fact, anything that is not given as a result of love is not truly a gift.

The gift of God is eternal life, and this does not mean simply living forever. It means living forever in a state of being fully alive. As sin brings death to the soul, so God's gift (Christians call it Grace) brings life to the soul. Sin kills relationships; Grace restores them. Sin kills a community; Grace rebuilds it. Sin kills our bodies and our souls; Grace gives them eternal life, and abundant life – full life, rich life, and vibrant life.

So then, if we've earned the paycheck, but we want the gift, what is the step forward? How do we get from our paycheck to God's gift? Through Jesus Christ, our Lord.

Jesus died on the cross as an atonement for our sins – as a setting-right, as a step to reconciliation, as a means to make us "at one" with God. If we accept His gift of eternal life, we are set right with God. We can allow His Grace to fill our lives and to make us truly alive.

This is distinct from the teachings of other world religions in two very important ways. Some world religions teach that the accumulation of good deeds – in the pantheistic family of religions, this would be good karma – can outweigh the evil deeds that one has committed. Others teach that nothing can be done about our evil, and that we must embrace our nature, regardless whether its moral bias leans towards good or evil. "The swan does not need a daily washing to remain white, nor the crow a daily inking to remain black," is a statement attributed to Lao Tzu, founder of Taoism, in a legendary dialog with Confucius, founder of Confucianism.

Most religions have something to say about morality, usually a recitation of moral rules, or possibly a passage on the importance of keeping moral rules. Religions which teach karmic balance (Hinduism and Buddhism, as two examples) teach that sins will be punished, possibly in a future lifetime, and encourage good deeds to counterbalance them.

Pre-Christian polytheism in Egypt taught something similar; that the hearts of the dead were weighed and must be found "light as a feather." Zoroastrianism, likewise, teaches a judgment of the soul after death, based on a balance of one's deeds.

Only Christianity teaches that immoral acts can be not merely outweighed, but actually cured. Christianity teaches that the penitent human, having accepted God's free gift of grace, is not merely forgiven of sin, but held blameless, as if the sin had never occurred.

In a very noteworthy passage from the prophet Isaiah, we read this call to reconciliation:

> *"Come, let us counsel together, says the LORD: Though your sins be as scarlet, they shall be whiter than snow; though they be red like crimson, they shall be as wool."*
> – Isaiah 1:18

The treatment for immorality – the cure for sin – does not result from good deeds. It instead results from an atoning act of

Jesus of Nazareth. Note the first point of the pre-Pauline doctrine: That Jesus Christ died for the sins of humankind.

Some are quick to point out other so-called gods who are said to have died, such as Osirus or Baldur. But no one has ever claimed that Osirus or Baldur died for someone else's crimes. Christianity teaches that Jesus of Nazareth died for the sole purpose of atoning for the sins of any human willing to follow Him.

In the New Testament book of Hebrews, we find a startling concept: Jesus, the High Priest. A priest is someone who mediates between a god and a human. Jesus, we teach, mediates between God and Mankind, but Jesus is also that God with whom He mediates, and He is the sacrifice that He offers to Himself. Imagine Jesus, as God, receiving Jesus, the sacrifice, offered by Jesus the High Priest.

No other religion features a god who lays aside his glory, mingles with his creations, befriends them, acts as a servant to them, and then allows himself to be tortured to death in the most horrible and humiliating of fashions, all in order to win them new life. In this teaching, Christianity is distinct from all others.

We might digress at this point, and distinguish Christianity further by the fact that while other religions claim that their gods did miraculous things in some indistinct unknowable dreamtime history, Christianity makes its claims in an actual documented time. It contains distinct touchstones that correlate to external historical documents. In later chapters, we will discuss some of those.

So we've looked at the gospel – the basic teaching of Christianity – in two very simple ways: The pre-Pauline gospel (You can find Paul's description of it in 1 Corinthians 15) and the Roman Road. That's Christianity in a nutshell.

As a child, I was taught that the most important verse of the Bible was John 3:16:

> *"For God so loved the world that He gave His only begotten son, that whosoever believes on Him shall not perish, but have eternal life."*

As an adult, it is my belief that Romans 6:23 is a much clearer explanation of the faith:

> *"For the wages of sin is death, but the gift of God is eternal life, through Jesus Christ our Lord."*

There are other simple explanations of Christianity: *"Man broke it, God fixed it"* is one of them. But there's more to Christianity than this. So let's look at a few more things about basic Christianity.

Central to Christianity is a man named Jesus of Nazareth and a book called the New Testament. It is an understatement to say that no man and no book have ever been more misunderstood than this book and this man.

In one of the books of the New Testament, Luke quotes a Roman official, Festus, who is trying to explain to another Roman official just what the Gospel is all about, and why Paul is in jail. He says it like this:

> *"It has something to do with their Jewish laws, and with some man named Jesus, who died, but whom Paul asserts to be alive."*
> – Acts 25:19

Well, that is the gospel in a nutshell, but some pieces are missing. Paul did assert that Jesus died, and that He rose again. I also assert this. Festus failed to understand why Jesus died, or how He came back to life. Even in Paul's day, the gospel Paul taught was being misunderstood.

So let's begin with what the book contains, and what it does not contain.

The New Testament is an anthology of 27 books. Some are very short – less than a page. Others are long, but not by the standards of modern books.

The first four books are biographies of Jesus. Three of these are attributed to His friends and followers. One of them is a compilation of events resulting from interviews with many people who knew Him. The first account –that is, the oldest; it is second in the anthology – is that of John Mark, and it is called the Gospel According to Mark, or simply "Mark."

John Mark was a follower of Paul, and later of Barnabas, and finally of Peter. Peter was one of Jesus' best friends. Tradition tells us that John Mark wrote the gospel as Peter dictated it to him. There is evidence to support this: mentions of John Mark in Paul's letters and Luke's histories associate Peter and Mark; and in another place Peter is described as being poorly educated, and thus in need of a scribe. Also, Mark's gospel does not mention any of the more embarrassing things that Peter did, which suggests that the writer did not wish to expose Peter to ridicule.

Matthew's gospel was written by Matthew, also called Levi. He was a disciple of Jesus and followed him closely. His account was written to show how the prophecies in the older Jewish writings were fulfilled by Jesus.

Luke was a follower of Paul, and as a result encountered many people who had seen the life of Jesus Christ or had followed Him in person. His account is the longest and most detailed. It continues in a second book, the Acts of the Apostles.

John is the last book of the four, and the last to be written. John takes a different approach, and tells us anecdotes about Jesus instead of attempting to write a more traditional biography. While his gospel covers the period of Jesus' ministry in a roughly chronological order, he does not try to fit it into a definite time-line.

John's gospel is the easiest for a modern reader to pick up and read through. If you were planning to read the New Testament, John's gospel is the place to begin.

So what do the gospels tell us about this Jesus of Nazareth?

They tell us the story of a Jewish man who lived in a Jewish community in the first century, and who observed the Jewish Law and its traditions. He lived for thirty years and then began teaching the people around Him. He did this for three years, and then was placed on trial for blasphemy in the Jewish courts, and for rebellion in the Roman courts. He was convicted and executed.

And on the third day – that is, about 36 hours after He was executed – He rose from the dead and visited with His disciples.

There's much more to it than that, of course.

Matthew and Luke both describe Jesus' birth. Luke begins by telling us about the birth of Jesus' cousin, John the Baptist. He then talks about Mary, Jesus' mother, having a vision that she was to bear a child, and going to visit with her cousin, Elizabeth, who was already six months pregnant with John the Baptist.

Matthew tells us about Mary's dilemma: She was engaged to be married, and she was suddenly pregnant. This was a very dangerous thing. Her husband had the right to have her killed for adultery.

Fortunately, Joseph was a very gentle man, and decided that instead of exposing her to shame or having her killed, that he would just quietly end the engagement and allow her to do as she pleased – perhaps to marry the baby's father. As he slept one night, he saw a vision that informed him of the child's origin, and that instructed him to take Mary as his bride, so he did.

Luke tells us that while Mary was very pregnant, about to give birth, there was a census taken, and Joseph had to return to the city where he was born, Bethlehem. * There, Jesus was born. We celebrate Jesus' birth at Christmas, but nothing in the Bible says that he was born in December. In fact, it is far more likely that he was born in June of 1 BC.

Luke tells us of Shepherds who were alerted to the birth by angels, and of wise men from the east who observed movements of the stars and followed them to Jerusalem, then to Bethlehem, seeking the King of the Jews.

This came as a shock to Herod the Great, who, according to the Roman authorities, was the King of the Jews, and who had seen no recent births in his family. **

He consulted the scribes, and based on Micah 5:2, sent the stargazers to Bethlehem. Following the visit of the wise men, Joseph had another vision, and as a result took his family into Egypt.

Herod suspected that a child in Bethlehem – the birthplace of a famous King from about 1000 BC, King David – was being raised and groomed to overthrow Herod's rule. To prevent this, Herod ordered the murder of every child in Bethlehem under the age of two years. This is sometimes called the slaughter of the innocents.

After Herod's death, Joseph returned to Israel and moved to Nazareth, in the extreme North of that small country. There, he raised Jesus as his own son.

Luke describes another incident of Jesus' youth: When he was about twelve years old, he went with his parents to Jerusalem. It was the custom for all Jews to visit Jerusalem for three festivals every year, and this was such an occasion. In the large group that were travelling to Jerusalem and returning to the North, Jesus was overlooked. It is very likely that his parents assumed he was walking with friends, or walking among other relatives.

As they stopped for the evening meal, Mary and Joseph discovered Jesus missing and searched for him. In desperation, they returned to Jerusalem, where they found Him in the temple, sitting with the priests and the teachers of the law, who were amazed at his wisdom and knowledge. When Mary and Joseph chided him from not returning with them, He said, "Didn't you know that I would be in My Father's house?"

From this event – one imagines that Luke heard this from Mary's own mouth – there is nothing else about Jesus' life until His baptism.

In the fifteenth year of Tiberius, Luke tells us – and this would have been about 29 or 30 AD, as we know from secular sources that Tiberius became Caesar in 14 AD – Jesus encountered his cousin, John the Baptist. John had become a hermit of sorts, and had begun to teach that people needed repentance. He started a ritual known as Baptism – we can find no earlier reference to it – and he instructed people to come back to the Jordan River and to be dipped into it as a sign of starting over.

It was an historical reference to the crossing of the Jordan River by Joshua, when the Israelites first entered Canaan and conquered it, in about 1280 BC. John was teaching that they had strayed far from that original devotion, and that a new immersion in the river was needed as a new starting place.

All four gospels tell of Jesus coming to the Jordan to be baptized. Mark and John begin their gospels with this event.

As Jesus rose from the water, a dove descended upon His head and a loud voice was heard, proclaiming Him to be God's Son. John began to declare Him to be the "Lamb of God, who takes away the sins of the world." John announced that while He had baptized with water, Jesus would baptize with the Holy Spirit.

Throughout the Jewish writings, the Holy Spirit of God – God's breath or God's ghost – would descend upon an individual and allow that individual to do miracles. An historical hero, Samson, was described as pulling down a pagan temple with his bare hands while the Holy Spirit was upon him. The legendary figure King David, under the influence of the Breath of God, fought off armies, and then danced ecstatically in front of the visible symbols of God's presence.

Thus, when the New Testament tells us of the Holy Spirit descending onto Jesus in the form of a dove, and of Jesus being one who would baptize with the Holy Spirit, these are not merely pious blessings. This is a literal claim that Jesus would perform miracles, and that others would perform miracles through Jesus.

John was essentially declaring that Jesus was God in the flesh.

We have to back up here, and understand some things from the Jewish writings – the Tanakh, as the Jews call it, or the Old Testament, as Christians call it. In the Tanakh, there are many references – prophecies – to a coming King, who would be God in the flesh. One of the earliest is in Genesis, when humanity sinned, but God declared that a descendant of Eve would crush the head of the serpent (sin).

In Numbers, the fourth book of the Tanakh, a prophet was summoned by a king and ordered to curse the Israelites. Instead, the prophet discovered that only blessings would come out of his mouth, and in the middle of these, he suddenly said, *"More: I see Him, but not near; Coming, but not now." (Num 24:17)*

In one of the books of poetry, a desperate man named Job suddenly declares, *"I know that my Redeemer lives, and that He shall stand upon this earth upon the last day; I shall see Him with my own eyes, even if my flesh has been buried and has decomposed."* Again and again, people in the Tanakh suddenly had flashes that there would come a King – A suffering servant, a successor to Mighty King David, and a leader who would be like God – or even would be God Himself. These messianic references are found throughout the Tanakh.

David, the great King of the Golden Age of Judaism, wrote this in Psalm 110:1, 3:

> *"The LORD said to my Lord, sit at my right hand until I have made thine enemies a footstool beneath thy feet … Thou art a priest forever, declares the LORD, and will not change His mind: Thou art a priest forever, after the order of Melchizedek."*

Jesus used this prophecy in one of his arguments with the religious leaders of His day, asking, "If the Messiah will be David's son, how will He also be David's Lord?"

John, in declaring Jesus to be the Lamb of God, and the one who would take away the sins of the world, marks Jesus as the Messiah – the expected King from the ancient Jewish writings. And after John declared Jesus to be the Lamb of God, that's when things became interesting, according to the gospels.

From the Baptism of Jesus onwards, the gospels tell us of Jesus doing miracles. They all agree that he taught with amazing wisdom; that He healed the sick; that He gave sight, hearing and restoration to the blind, the deaf, and the maimed. He healed lepers.

But Jesus did not merely heal physical ailments. He also addressed spiritual, social, and mental issues. He is credited with healing a wild man in the region known as Gad – the "Gadarene Demoniac" – and with causing the man to sit peacefully, dress himself according to social norms, and to speak calmly. The gospels describe Jesus conversing with evil spiritual entities – demons – and ordering them to leave humans whom they had possessed.

Some in the modern world interpret this to mean that Jesus treated mental illness, and discount the literal descriptions of demonic actions. Others take the demonic references at face value. In either case, Jesus restored the mental function that the man had lost, according to the gospel accounts.

In another instance – the woman at the well, in John 4 – Jesus used a woman's social stigmas to heal her of deep psychological traumas, and to restore her place in her society – a place she had lost through sexual promiscuity.

Jesus taught people to be physically, mentally, and spiritually healthy. An excellent example of this occurs in the Sermon on the Mount (Matthew chapters 5 through 8) in which Jesus teaches that happiness arises from sorrow, and that one must not worry about things that one cannot change. He taught that a healthy outlook, and viewing the world with an untainted eye, is vital to happiness – "The eye is the window of the soul." He taught that looking at the world as it is, without lenses of depression or anger, will provide light to the soul and yield a healthy outlook on life.

But Jesus primarily taught about Himself. He read a messianic prophecy from the Tanakh in one synagogue meeting. Then he told the congregation that, "Today, in your presence, these things are fulfilled." – that is, that He was this King, this Suffering Servant, and this God Incarnate whom they had expected.

To the woman at the well, in John 4, He was even more direct: when she mentioned the coming Messiah, He replied, "I, who speak to you, am He."

At a festival involving the lighting of lamps in recognition of the glory of God, He stood among the lamp stands and yelled out, "I am the Light of the World."

At a festival celebrating water that had sustained Moses and the Israelites in the desert – an historical event from about 1300 BC – As the priest poured the water, Jesus shouted, "If any man is thirsty, let him come to me and drink."

When the Jewish leaders argued with Him, and Abraham their common ancestor was mentioned, Jesus claimed that He had seen Abraham, and that Abraham had rejoiced to see Jesus. Since the historical figure of Abraham had lived in about 1700 or 1800 BC, the leaders scoffed at the idea that Jesus had spoken with Abraham. It would be like you or I speaking with King Arthur or with the Roman Emperor Constantine. But when they laughed at Him, Jesus replied, "Before Abraham was, I Am."

The absolute audacity of this claim cannot be overstated. "I Am" was considered to be the holy name of God, written as four unpronounceable letters (YHWH or JHVH) to prevent it from being spoken aloud and thus potentially profaned. Jesus not only said the unspeakable name of God, but He used it with reference to Himself. And He used it to back the claim that He had seen Abraham in person, which could only be possible if He were much more than human.

The Jews took up stones with which to stone him to death, because they correctly interpreted this as a claim of deity. Jesus had just said, in so many words, that He was God in the flesh. There could be no more blasphemous statement than this in their minds.

This event, and one other event, led the Jewish leaders to decide that Jesus must die. The other event is in John chapter 11. Again, Jesus claims deity in the form of claiming power over life and death. He says, in vv. 25-26:

"I am the resurrection and the life. He who believes in me, though he were dead, yet shall he live. Whoever believes in me and lives shall never die."

If that were not enough, Jesus then raised a dead man – a man who had been dead for four days; long enough that he was not merely stunned or perhaps drugged, but who had begun to stink of decomposition. In the old King James Version of this passage, John quotes the dead man's sister as saying, "He hath been in the grave four days, and he stinketh."

But on Jesus' command, John tells us, Lazarus came out of the tomb, and had to be cut loose from his grave-wrappings.

Even when he was being judged by Pilate, Jesus confirmed that He claimed to be a King, and then added, "My kingdom is not of this world." Those who heard this understood Him to mean that He was a spiritual King, that is, God.

It is unavoidable that Jesus claimed to be God. We cannot escape this fact about Him. His teachings all carry this single theme, beneath and above all else. We can argue about the truth-value of this claim, but we cannot escape this claim.

And this leads us to the single biggest problem about Jesus: That He claimed He was God. G.K. Chesterton, and later C.S. Lewis, both wrote passages about what this means. In very simple terms, Jesus of Nazareth was either a very evil man, worse than the worst madmen and dictators who have left their blemishes upon history, or else He was the very best of all possible men: God in the flesh.

What we cannot say is that Jesus was merely a good man, or that he was simply an historical figure. He was evil, or He was God. It is a binary choice.

Those who believed Him to be an evil man brought about His death. He was accused of blasphemy, and if He was not God, then this charge was true. He did claim to be God, and He did claim and exercise authority that belongs to God Alone. He did things that only God was allowed to do, such as forgiving the sins of the people whom He healed. But those who accused him lacked the power to execute him, so a serious charge under Roman law had to be made against Him.

He was accused of revolution against the Roman Empire, and this charge was false. Nonetheless, it was the one for which He was executed, and in a particularly painful manner reserved for the worst criminals.

One must pause at this point to dispel some rumors. Some have suggested that Jesus survived crucifixion by various means.

One rumor is that a disciple was crucified in His place, and that He escaped. There are very large problems with this theory, the first being that His disciples were accounted for following the crucifixion. The second is that this theory first arises several centuries after the event.

Another persistent rumor is that Jesus was crucified, but somehow survived the event. Those who support this theory simply do not understand crucifixion. Crucifixion was not meant to be a humane method of killing criminals. It was meant to be an example to others who contemplated the same sorts of crimes. It was designed to be cruel, painful, bloody, and horrifying brutal, as befitted, in the Roman mind, rebels, revolutionaries, and those who challenged the power of Rome. It was meant as a manifesto: "Take us on and we'll do the same to you!"

The prisoner to be killed was first beaten. This whipping with the cat-of-nine-tails was known as the forty-minus-one: Forty stripes was almost always lethal, so the punishment stopped at thirty-nine. Despite this restraint, the mortality rate for Roman scourging was about 12.5%. Those who survived it and were then released were often permanently maimed, and seldom regained their former strength.

A scourge – a long leather whip with many strands, each of which was studded with bits of stone, metal beads, and animal bones – would be applied in rotation to the left, to the right, and in the center of the victim's back. The embedded material would penetrate and flay skin and muscle, tearing it from the body. Thirteen such cycles, thirty-nine strokes in all, completed the punishment. It was not uncommon for rib bones and vertebrae to be exposed.

Blood loss, risk of infection, and the simple shock of such an intensely painful event significantly raised the short-term odds of death after the scourging. But for the crucified, this was merely the first stage. In Jesus' case, due to the proximity of an important holiday, his trial lasted all night and led directly to his execution the following morning. In the interim, he was further beaten with fists – imagine boxing movies, and the punishment that a boxer endures. But Jesus could not even defend Himself.

To add insult to injury, He was given a crown of thorns to wear, to mock His alleged royal aspirations. Those who tried to lead rebellions were shown no mercy at all.

At this point, his back was virtually destroyed, his face puffy and purple, with blood on his face from the thorns and the beatings; his facial hair ripped out in chunks – it would have been hard to recognize his face as that of a human. One of the prophets, seeing this event in advance, wrote that his face was more marred than any man.

Without rest, He was given a large wooden cross to carry on his shoulders. The muscles of his back, which might otherwise have supported such a load, had already been ripped away by the scourge. His shoulders would have been bleeding and sore. To walk was agony; to carry a heavy wooden cross was beyond excruciating. But Roman tradition made the condemned carry the cross.

In Jesus' case, the gospels state that He was unable to carry the cross, and that the Romans forced a passerby to carry it for Him. But that was only the second stage of the punishment. On reaching the place of execution, He was nailed to the cross. A nail went through each wrist, and another passed through His ankles, among the metatarsal bones. This would have been bloody, intensely painful, and potentially deadly on its own – think of those who have cut their wrists in hopes of dying – but it was only the third stage of the punishment.

The worst, and final, stage of the punishment came once the crucified, suspended by nails – some offenders were merely tied to crosses with ropes, but Jesus was nailed on – was placed upright. With the arms above the chest, drawing breath required pushing one's feet downward, scraping one's mangled back along the rough wood, and inhaling through a bloody face. Then the pain of the pierced feet would force the crucified to sag, putting the weight onto the nails through the wrists, again scraping his back along the rough wood. This action would repeat, breath by breath, without relief.***

After several hours, or sometimes after several days of drawing one agonizing breath after another through this excruciating cycle, Roman soldiers would break the legs of the accused, thus preventing them from drawing a full breath. Death by suffocation would occur within minutes afterwards. If there were any doubt as to the death of the crucified, the Roman soldiers would use other weapons to administer a killing blow.

A Roman dared not be wrong about the death of a prisoner. To allow escape was to take on the punishment of the one who escaped. It is safe to say that no crucified person survived the punishment, simply based on the unthinkable cost of the executioner being wrong.

In the case of Jesus, after He was discovered to be dead from suffocation, the Romans did not break His legs, but instead made an upward thrust with a spear into his side. This would have passed through His lungs, liver, and heart, at the very least. Had he been in perfect health at that moment, it is still inevitable that the thrust of the spear would have killed Him.

To believe that He might have survived to this point is absolutely unrealistic. But if we suspend our disbelief and assume that He was somehow alive when He was taken down from the cross, the very worst possible treatment for His injuries would be to place him on a cold stone shelf in a cave, closed off from light and air. But that is what happened to him next. Two of His followers – not even His closest friends, but merely two followers – begged for His body, wrapped him with spices and perfumes, as was customary, and placed Him into a tomb.

Imagine a man who had been scourged in the Roman style, had dragged an immense wooden cross up a steep hill, had suffered life-threatening penetration wounds of his wrists and ankles, had suffocated on a cross for at least three hours, had suffered a spear wound to his side at an upward angle, and then had been left in a cold dark cave for 36 hours. Imagine how much blood those accumulated injuries would have drained from Him. Now imagine that he was somehow still alive.

There are those who will say, without so much as a blink to suggest that they understand how ridiculous such a thing truly is, that Jesus was stunned, perhaps even maimed; that He swooned on the cross, and did not die. They do not stop to think that for any human being to survive so many deadly events would be akin to Louis XVI, freshly beheaded, taking up his severed head and carrying it off into the sunset. But to those who would deny the resurrection, logic has no place.

Nonetheless, let us pretend with them that Jesus survived the cross, then 36 hours in a cold, dark tomb, and finally, Sunday morning, stumbled out into the light, where a disciple saw Him before He finally collapsed into another grave, dead for good and all. Anyone seeing such a man would think he was dead. His face and body would be maimed. He would probably be unable to stand upright or to walk. No one would see him and say that they had seen a living being, even if they recognized him.

But Jesus, according to the gospels, was seen alive about 36 hours after His death. Witnesses – there were as many as 500 at one event – claim that He was not merely healthy, but radiant. Two witnesses claim that He walked a day's journey with them to a nearby town called Emmaus. It would seem obvious that a man who could not carry a cross up a hill on Friday would be in no shape to walk seven miles on Sunday. In two separate events, He entered a locked room and shared a meal with ten of His disciples, and then with eleven of them.

The gospels end with Jesus ordering His disciples to teach others about what they had seen and heard. They clearly and unequivocally declared that He died, and that there were no doubts about it; and that He rose out of His grave, where He was seen by many; as many as 500 at one time. If the gospels are to be believed at all, then this one claim must be seen as part and parcel of that claim, inseverable from his moral teachings and the story of His life.

Luke, the historian, continues in a second book, called Acts of the Apostles, and records what the disciples of Jesus did after Jesus returned to heaven.

That is the life of Jesus, as the gospels share it with us. Do not take my word for it. Read the book of John, and see for yourself. I have left out many parts, including the teachings of Jesus. We will address those in Stage 1.

For now, our goal was to lay out, in the broadest of terms, what Christians believe and teach. We have done that. The pre-Pauline doctrine taught that Jesus died for the sins of humankind, was buried, rose on the third day, was seen by many, and shall return again. The Roman road explains that we are sinners; that sin leads to death; that God loves us and offers us eternal life; and that eternal life is available to those who confess Jesus as Lord, and believe that God has raised Him from the dead.

We also discussed the life of Jesus, in general and broad terms.

Hopefully, this answers the first big question about Christianity, specifically, what Christianity is all about.

Endnotes:

* This leads us to a problem known as the Quirinian problem. Luke tells us that Quirinius (Cyrenius) was the governor of Syria – the Romans considered Syria to cover the entire area – and that this was the first census taken during that period. Josephus, in his *Antiquities of the Jews,* tells us that Quirinius was made governor of Syria in a year that we would call 6 AD.

There have since been discovered other monuments and inscriptions referring to a census taken under Quirinius in about 1 BC. These inscriptions also point to Quirinius having been made a ceremonial governor of Syria much earlier than Josephus would have us believe – Josephus is describing a later event, when Quirinius was made the full official governor of the region.

** Thus we come to the Herodian problem. According to Josephus, Herod the Great lived until about 4 BC. Here, we see him in about 1 or 2 AD ordering the slaughter of the innocents.

This is also a problem that can be resolved. Nearly all printed copies of Josephus' Antiquities of the Jews are reprints of the 1523 edition. This edition, the first to be taken from hand-copied manuscripts and printed by press, was translated and printed in large volumes. Unfortunately, it contains an error of translation. In the oldest manuscripts of Josephus', Herod lived until about 1 or 2 AD, depending on which lunar eclipse Josephus meant.

Luke clearly means to tell us that Jesus was born in the year that would later be known as 1 BC. He tells us that in the fifteenth year of Tiberius (29-30 AD) Jesus was about 30 years old (Luke 3:23). I will leave the reader to do the math.

*** There was also the process of inverted crucifixion, with the cross placed like an X on the ground. In this variant, as with the "normal" crucifixion, the victim was unable to breathe properly due to positional asphyxia. Inverted, the abdomenal organs would lay upon the diaphragm, preventing it from flexing. Eventually, the victim could no longer force air from his lungs.

Tradition states that Peter was crucified thus.

Portrait of a Stage Zero Christian:
(Cf. John's gospel, chapter 4)

She lived in a small town in the bad part of the country. Her people were considered half bloods, traitors, and apostate heretics. Among their other faults, they didn't practice the "true faith" of the people who lived to the north and south of them.

Even in her own town, she was an outcast. She had a bad reputation, because after several failed marriages, she had given up on marriage and lived with a man to whom she wasn't married. She had no friends, because the local women didn't trust her. She had lovers, but no friends. Even the man with whom she lived – even he was not truly a friend, not as a spouse should be. Shame and fear of rejection made her keep silent about the things she had done. Friends were a luxury she could never afford. No one could be allowed to see into her soul.

Because she was ashamed to be in the company of reputable women, she didn't go to the well in the early mornings, when it was cool. She went to the well in the middle of the day, when she was certain she wouldn't see anyone she knew. Carrying heavy water jugs in the heat of the day was less painful than talking to the local women.

One day, there was a man at the well. In her culture, men didn't speak to women they didn't know. And they especially didn't speak to her kind of women – not unless they wanted something shameful. This man, by his clothing, was not even from her people. He was from one of the pureblooded tribes to the north or the south.

But he spoke to her.

"Please," he said, "May I have some water when you have drawn it?"

"Your people want nothing to do with us, and won't even drink out of cups we use," she replied. "And you're a man. Should you really be asking me for water?" She hoped to shame him, and thus to hide her own shame.

"If you knew the gift God gives, and who asks you for water, you would have asked me for living water."

She smirked. "This well is deep, and you don't have any means of drawing water. So where will you get this living water? I suppose that you're greater than our ancestor, who dug this well?"

"Whoever drinks from this well will become thirsty again later. But whoever drinks the water that I give will never thirst again: There will be a spring of living water inside his very soul."

She smiled, careful to mock him only slightly. "Well, by all means, give me this water. Then I won't have to come back to this well." And even though she was mocking Him, that thought pleased her, because of the shame in drawing water when no one was around. If she could be freed of that shame… But it couldn't be true. He was playing with her. So she would just play along.

"First," he said, "Go get your husband and bring him back here."

That wiped the smile from her face. "Sir, I don't have a husband.".

"That's true," he said. "You've had five husbands, and the man you're living with isn't your husband."

How did He know that? Who had told Him? "I see that you are some kind of a prophet," she said, trying to change the subject. "Maybe you can answer a religious question for me. We don't worship God the way that you do: what is the right way to worship? Is it ours or yours?"

"God is a spirit," He replied, "And those who truly worship Him are those who worship in spirit and in truth."

"Well," she said, content that they were no longer talking about her shame, "When the Messiah comes, God's great messenger, He will explain it all to us."

"I am that One," he said. "I, who now speak to you, am that Messiah."

Consider what happened here: A woman, minding her own business, met the Creator God in the flesh: Jesus of Nazareth. He forced her to face her shame, and then He took it away. Many people in the Samaritan town of Sychar came to believe on Jesus – to believe that He was the Messiah, the Son of God. She was the first, the one who found Him, and the one who brought the others to Him.

Through this chance encounter, she went from being an outcast in her society to being a treasured member of a new society, formed around Jesus. This is what it means to be a Stage Zero Christian: Admitting that we have sinned, and asking Jesus to heal that sin. We offer him our shame, and He does not condemn us, but gives us honor in its place.

STAGE ONE
Living the Faith

LIVING THE FAITH consists primarily of two disciplines, which are prayer and the reading of the Bible. Of course it's not that simple, and yet, it actually is that simple.

Prayer, in the Christian faith, is different from prayer in most other faiths. It does not consist of the recitation of certain prescribed texts (though it can be done that way). It is instead intended as a dialog between a believer and the Creator. Jesus gave us examples of a dialog sort of prayer – It would be a very worthwhile study to go through the New Testament and to note the prayers of Jesus.

Likewise, reading the Bible is different from simply reading through a book and then setting it aside. The Bible is meant to be a textbook from which the reader continually draws new knowledge and accepts new challenges. The Bible is meant to be read very often and very well.

After you have read this book that you now hold in your hands, you may well put it on a shelf and never touch it again, or perhaps you may lend it to a friend. The Bible is different: It will be most effective if it is read daily. You may read the same passage repeatedly, each time gaining a new insight into the verses. Or you may read various parts that interconnect – for example, linking the letters by Paul with the journeys in Acts of the Apostles, where those cities are mentioned.

The Bible was meant to be studied – to be carefully combed through. To be made part of our lives. To be absorbed. To become one with us.

There is a bit of a paradox in Bible reading as a means to grow your faith: The Bible contains some difficult passages. These are not parts that are hard to read but rather, parts that are hard to understand and to put into context. Many people in the Bible – even principal characters, whom we might consider heroes or great persons of faith – do things that are simply awful.

Anti-theists – I make a distinction here between an atheist who simply does not believe the Bible, and an anti-theist, who is opposed to having anyone believe the Bible – often point to the difficult passages and try to ridicule the Bible as a result. "Oh," they say, "Your Bible has heroes like King David, who committed adultery, then covered it up by committing murder."

Well, they are correct. All of the heroes in the Bible except Jesus are flawed and sinful human beings. We will address some of these difficult passages in later chapters. For now, simply understand two lessons that these difficult passages teach us.

First, all human beings are flawed by their very nature. We discussed this in chapter one, when we talked about the Roman Road. Second, the Bible writers expected the readers to know right from wrong – that is, to have a moral compass already aligned with the Law of Moses.

Because the Bible writers assumed that everyone knew it was wrong to murder, they do not attach a moral judgement to the descriptions of murder in the Bible. When David kills Uriah (by proxy) you are expected to already know that this was a grave sin against God and against Uriah (not to mention Bathsheba and the Nation of Israel). When David commits adultery, you are expected to understand already that this was evil, and that he knew better.

David's sin with Bathsheba and the later sin of murdering Uriah are not the most difficult passages in the Bible, by any stretch of the imagination. Many people who appear in the Bible commit many evil deeds. But as you come to understand the Bible more thoroughly, you will come to understand why the difficult passages are there.

Through David and Bathsheba, we come to understand that even a murderer can be forgiven and can have a restored relationship with God. An adulterous wife can be reconciled to God, and from her there may arise a line of kings. And there is a deeper principle as well. If every person in the Bible except Jesus is a dirty rotten sinner, who cannot keep the Law of Moses, then we need something better and more powerful than a set of laws. We need something that is above offerings of bullocks and goats and lambs and turtledoves. We need Grace.

We will talk more about Grace in later chapters. For now, it is important to remember that the Bible contains difficult passages, but that we must trust God to give us an understanding of these passages. We must also keep in mind that every human, including the great heroes of the Bible, are sinners who must be saved by Grace. And finally, we must remember that the Bible writers expected us to know right from wrong.

So why do we have those difficult passages in the Bible?

I can't give you a definitive answer to that, but I can tell you that there are two recurring and concurrent themes in those horrible passages. The first is that when we follow God's laws and put Him first, our lives may not be perfect, but they will make sense. The second is that when we "do what is right in our own eyes" (Judges 17:6, Judges 21:25, Proverbs 21:2) we wind up doing stupid, evil, sinful things that seemed right at the time.

Proverbs 14:12 warns us that "There is a way that seems right unto a man, but the end thereof is death," and the passages in which people acted on their own ideas of right and wrong demonstrate clearly that this proverb is true. Even today, in our world... But we digress.

With those starting points established, let's look at the more practical aspects. In appendix B (for Bible) of this book, there is an outline of the Bible. I would encourage you to read through that outline and understand the general story of the Bible. Then, as you read the Bible from day to day, you will be able to put the parts into context – you can place them on the outline, so that you see the bigger picture.

The Bible is one big picture, but it is drawn by placing many smaller pictures into a single frame, like a mosaic composed of mosaics composed of mosaics. One of my favorite books in the Bible is a book called Ruth, which tells the story of a family in around 1100 BC. This book not only tells us about a brave and gracious woman named Ruth, but it also gives us a glimpse of the nature of God. And at the same time, it is a bit of the story of the nation of Israel. And it is a small part of the ongoing story of how Jesus came to redeem us.

Each book of the Bible fits into the bigger context, and is interwoven with all of the others. Each part of the Bible stands on its own, and yet, it makes the most sense when it is fitted into its place. The intricacies of the Bible, and the profound links within it, are worthy of an entire book of their own.

Once you have this outline of the Bible established in your mind, at least loosely, then begin to read specific parts of the Bible. I recommend starting with the Gospel of John. John was Jesus' closest earthly friend, and spent the most time with Jesus. He tells the life of Jesus as a series of short stories or anecdotes, each linked and yet distinct, like the Bible itself.

The Gospel of John also addresses many heretical ideas that arose in the first couple of centuries. For example, there were folks who believed that Jesus was not really God. John affirms that Jesus was God. There were people who believed that Jesus was not really human. John affirms that Jesus was human. John affirms that Jesus created the universe. John declares that Jesus came to bring light into the dark places of the human heart. All of the errors that a person might make about Jesus are corrected in John.

Once you have read John's gospel, I would encourage you to continue and read Acts, the very next book. This book, by Luke, tells what the early believers did after Jesus returned to Heaven. It describes their beliefs, their practices, and even their disagreements. It talks about the difficulties of being a Christian in a non-Christian world. It tells us how the early church reached out into the dark world around them, and how that world reacted – it even tells how the world misunderstood them.

From Acts of the Apostles, continue into Romans, and read Paul describing salvation, and why it was necessary, and what it means. Remember that we talked about Romans earlier, in discussing the Roman Road to salvation. Reading the entire book will help you to put those verses into the bigger picture.

Then back up, and read Matthew, Mark, and Luke. These will give you three slightly different views of the life of Jesus. They will explain what He taught, how he lived, and what He did. John told the story in short anecdotes, but the other gospel writers try to tell the story in order, from beginning to end.

Once you have read those books, God will have had a opportunity to speak to you through them. Just as prayer is primarily our messages to God, the Bible is primarily God's message to us. Both tools help us to communicate with God, but the two tools work best when used together.

We spoke earlier of prayer as a dialog. We need to express what we want God to know, and we need to listen for God to answer. A prayer can be a simple word or two in passing – "Lord help me" or "Lord, give that person strength" – and prayer can also be a lengthy discussion of our problems and of our thoughts.

In general, there are four types of prayer. We pray to give glory to God; we pray to thank God for things He has done; we pray to ask God for help; we pray to ask God to help others. Consider the model prayer that Jesus prayed when the disciples asked Him to teach them to pray.

First, He praised God: "Our Father, who art in Heaven, hallowed by Thy Name. Thy Kingdom come, Thy will be done, on Earth as it is in Heaven." (In modern English, *"God our Father in Heaven, Your name is holy. May we quickly see Your glory on Earth, in the same way that You are glorified in Heaven"*). Next He asked for personal needs, "Give us this day our daily bread... Forgive us our trespasses... Lead us not into temptation, but deliver us from evil." (*"Give us what we need for this day ... forgive us for our sins today ... protect us from the sin that we are drawn towards."*) Then He closed the prayer by praising God again: "For Thine is the Kingdom, and the power and the glory, forever and ever, amen." (*"For You are the King of all, and have all the power and the glory forever, as it should be."*)

In this prayer, Jesus did not thank God, but He did thank God in other prayers, such as His prayer just before raising Lazarus from the dead, in John 11. He also did not pray for others in this prayer, but He did pray for others – even you! – in John 17.

In both of these disciplines – prayer and Bible reading – start small and work your way up. It is better to pray for five minutes a day, and to read seven verses a week, than to promise yourself that you'll pray for hours and read the Bible cover to cover. Small goals that you meet are better than huge goals that you do not meet. Also, reading a few verses and thinking about them – trying to understand what they mean and what God wants you to understand from them – is better than reading huge passages and having only an overview of what they mean.

Prayer and Bible reading are much like physical exercise. The more that you do them, the more of them that you will be able to do. No one walks into a gym and lifts hundred of pounds on the first day. By lifting small weights repeatedly, a weightlifter builds up his strength. By reading small passages at a time, and praying a few minutes each day, a Christian builds his strength.

At first, your prayers may be short and awkward. "Um, God, you're, you know, really holy, and could you help me with my transportation issues?" Over time, your prayers will flow more naturally, and you will be able to open your heart to God. Likewise, as you become more familiar with the Bible, and begin to see how it all fits together, you will begin to see the larger picture of the one great story culminating in Jesus Christ.

At this point, you may be asking yourself if Bible reading and prayer are all that God expects of you. The short answer is, "No, of course not." But reading the Bible and praying daily will lead you to the passages that will show you what God expects of you. For example, suppose that you read Micah 6:8, *"But He has shown you, O Man, what is good, and what does the LORD require of you, except to act justly, to love mercy, and to be humble before your God?"*

In this, you see three things God expects:

1. Acting with justice
2. Loving mercy, that is, being merciful, and
3. Being humble before God.

Note that justice and mercy are two sides of one coin: One acts fairly towards others, and one forgives others who do not act fairly towards one. These two things, together, are how we are to treat others: With justice and mercy. The last thing is how we are to treat God: We are to approach Him in humility, that is, not with pride (what do we have to be proud of that is not a gift from God?) or with arrogance (do we believe ourselves stronger, more just, or more merciful than God?).

As you read this passage, you might feel a tug at your heart, and you might become aware that you have been unjust towards your neighbor. This may be the Spirit of God convicting you of sin, and expecting you to correct it. As you pray, you will sometimes feel a similar tugging at your spirit.

I must caution you that not all such tugging comes from God. The enemy will use guilt against you – this is why he is called "the accuser." There is, fortunately, a fairly simple way to know the source of such a feeling.

God convicts us to correct us. The accuser condemns us to destroy us. A feeling that I have wronged a brother or sister, and should speak to them to make it right, is likely to be a conviction from God. It tells me to act justly so that I can correct my error. But the accuser will tell me that I have failed, that I always fail, that such failures are impossible for me to overcome, and that I am helpless to make things right. These, of course, are lies, and are meant to make me ashamed or to destroy me.

I have a Christian brother who often speaks of "lie-based thinking." It consists, in a large part, of believing things that are not true – lies that we have been told until we believe them, and worse, act upon them. If I believe that I am no good, and cannot act justly, then I will quit trying to act justly, and the enemy will have won in my life. If I believe that I am shameful, and that others would be disgusted if they only knew about the dark places in my life, then I will not be able to open those dark places to the light – to confess what I've done wrong, and to try to make it right.

Instead, we must understand one important truth of the gospel: That Jesus knows our deepest and darkest secrets, and loves us in spite of them. There is no evil we cannot take to Him so that it can be made right, and we are truly capable of allowing God to act through us. We are capable, through Jesus, of acting justly, loving mercy, and walking humbly with our God.

This verse illustrates how God may use our prayers and our reading of the Bible to show us what He wants from us. God may point out to me that I have been unjust to my neighbor – I haven't paid back the $200 he lent to me. This causes me, through the prompting of the Holy Spirit, to walk across the street, knock on his door, and hand him the money. Now I have acted justly, and I have exposed what might have been a shameful thing to the light of the gospel, and I have made it right.

Instead, I could simply say, "Oh, I'm horrible that way; I always do that. I'm so disgusting." Then I might hide in my shame, avoid my neighbor, and eventually become angry with him, because every time I see him I am reminded of my own shame. That would be wrong. It would create a dark place in my heart, where the accuser can hide.

Because of this verse, and the prompting of the Spirit, I know that I am meant to make things right, and to be just instead of being shameful. There are other passages that tell us what God wants from us, as well, and let's look at how they match up with the passage in Micah 6:8.

There is a famous passage in Matthew's gospel, in which the religious leaders were trying to trick Jesus into saying something that would disgrace Him or discredit Him in front of his followers. One such trickster asked Jesus which commandment (of the ten commandments) was the greatest. No matter what He said, they would have a prepared argument to twist His words and make Him seem ignorant and silly.

But Jesus did not cite one of the ten commandments. He instead quoted a different part of the Torah, and said "As it is written, You must love the LORD your God with all your heart, and all your soul, and all your strength, and all your mind." (Matt. 22:37, cf. Deut. 10:11)

They had no response to this – they didn't expect Him to be able to answer at all. But Jesus went on and said, "And the second is like the first: Love your neighbor as you love yourself."

Micah told us to treat our neighbor with justice and mercy; Jesus tells us to love him as we love ourselves. Micah told us to walk humbly before God; Jesus tells us to love God with our entire being. See how these fit together. We see an excellent example of the internal consistency of the Bible: It all fits together.

But note that Jesus also raised the stakes from merely being merciful towards our neighbor. We are not to merely be merciful, or to perhaps help him out of a tight spot: We are to love our neighbor as ourselves. Loving one's neighbor sounds like a pleasant platitude until we see how much we love ourselves.

Do you ever allow yourself to go hungry? Do you ever allow yourself to go without clothing? Do you make yourself sleep outdoors in the rain? Or do you feed yourself, clothe yourself, and shelter yourself?

So the Bible draws us to another inescapable truth: That we are not capable, in our own strength, of doing what God expects of us. To be as good as God expects, and to love as He loves, we must be more than merely human. We must have the Son of God acting through us, we must be instruments of His Spirit, and we must have the hands of God attached to our merely human arms.

The Christian life is not merely as simple as reading the Bible and talking to God; It is also about allowing that conversation with God to affect how we live. It is about allowing the conviction of the

Holy Spirit to break our hearts, so that we can rebuild them as tools of God's mercy and power.

Earlier, we mentioned the ten commandments. These divide nicely into two parts: The first four commands deal with our relationship with God, and the last six deal with our relationship with other humans.

1. Have no other gods.
2. Make no idols to worship.
3. Use the Lord's name with respect.
4. Take one day per week to reserve for God.

5. Be respectful to your parents.
6. Do not give false testimony.
7. Do not commit adultery.
8. Do not murder.
9. Do not steal.
10. Do not desire another's belongings.

Jesus neatly summarized these: "Love the Lord with all your heart" and "Love your neighbor as yourself."

Note that these also fit into what Micah told us: If we act justly towards our neighbor, we will not lie about him, steal from him, or murder him. Justice and mercy for our parents requires offering them our respect, even if they don't deserve it (as some parents don't). Adultery and covetousness are both unjust, and interfere with our relationships with our neighbors.

What does it mean to be humble before God? Well, it might mean recognizing that there are no other gods; He and He alone, the only one of His kind, is the only true God. It would mean not making idols; John 4:24 tells us that God is a Spirit, and those who worship Him must worship in spirit and in truth. To be humble before God means not using His name as an incantation or a curse, and realizing that we cannot summon Him as we might call our dog. Taking a day to honor Him, and to rest from our labors; this too is humility before God.

Since we earlier mentioned the Lord's model prayer, let's see how well it matches with Micah 6:8:

Our Father, which art in Heaven, Hallowed be Thy Name.

Walking **humbly** with God by recognizing His greatness and submitting to His will

Thy Kingdom Come: Thy will be done, on earth as it in heaven.

Give us this day our daily bread, and forgive us our trespasses, as we forgive those who trespass against us.

Becoming **just** by asking forgiveness, and being **merciful** by forgiving others

And lead us not into temptation, but deliver us from evil. For Thine is the Kingdom, and the Power, and the Glory, forever. Amen.

Again, we **humbly** recognize God's greatness and our own weakness

All of these passages – The Old testament prophets, the Torah law, Jesus commands to His disciples, and the model prayer – come together to show us how to live the Christian life. Through the Bible and through prayer, we can apply these principles to our daily lives.

Some Stage 1 Teachings:

Let's look at some of Jesus' teachings, and examine what He said. Remember that in Stage 0, we only looked at the story that the disciples told about Jesus. Let's see some of the things that they quoted him as saying: *

Matthew 5:3-20:

3 Blessed [are] the poor in spirit: for theirs is the kingdom of heaven.
4 Blessed are they that mourn: for they shall be comforted.
5 Blessed are the meek: for they shall inherit the earth.
6 Blessed are they which do hunger and thirst after righteousness: for they shall be filled.
7 Blessed are the merciful: for they shall obtain mercy.
8 Blessed are the pure in heart: for they shall see God.
9 Blessed are the peacemakers: for they shall be called the children of God.
10 Blessed are they which are persecuted for righteousness' sake: for theirs is the kingdom of heaven.
11 Blessed are ye, when men shall revile you, and persecute you, and shall say all manner of evil against you falsely, for my sake.
12 Rejoice, and be exceeding glad: for great is your reward in heaven: for so persecuted they the prophets which were before you.

Note the same themes that we read in Micah 6:8. Jesus is teaching us to be **humble** before God (vv. 3, 4, 5), to be **just and righteous** (vv. 6, 8), and to be **merciful** (vv. 7,9). Then He gives a new teaching: That we should rejoice when we are unfairly treated for his sake, because the persecution of the righteous is a mark that they belong to God (vv. 10,11,12).

Keep in mind that this applies to persecution *"falsely, for my sake."* Jesus is not telling us that a righteous punishment for crimes that we have actually done honors God. He is telling us that to be unrighteously punished for belonging to God – to be falsely accused, attacked, and even killed in Jesus' name – brings glory to God.

> *13 Ye are the salt of the earth: but if the salt have lost his savour, wherewith shall it be salted? It is thenceforth good for nothing, but to be cast out, and to be trodden under foot of men.*

We sometimes stumble on this passage: How can salt "lose its savor?" Did the creator of the universe not understand the nature of sodium chloride?

To understand this, realize that salt in the first century was mined, often from the Dead Sea. It contained a large amount of impurities, such as sand or even dirt. Its usual use was to rub onto meat, giving flavor and preserving the meat. But as the actual salt seeped into the meat, the impurities would remain in the salt bin. Eventually, the salt itself, the pure sodium chloride, was used up, leaving only the impurities. This is "salt" that has "lost its savor." It was just sand and other minerals, and could only be thrown away.

> *14 Ye are the light of the world. A city that is set on an hill cannot be hid.*
> *15 Neither do men light a candle, and put it under a bushel, but on a candlestick; and it giveth light unto all that are in the house.*
> *16 Let your light so shine before men, that they may see your good works, and glorify your Father which is in heaven.*
>
> *17 Think not that I am come to destroy the law or the prophets: I am not come to destroy, but to fulfil.*
> *18 For verily I say unto you, Till heaven and earth pass, one jot or one tittle shall in no wise pass from the law, till all be fulfilled.*

This is an important teaching. Jesus did not change what the Jewish authorities taught. Even today, we accept the Torah – we accept the entire Tanakh (the "Old Testament") – exactly as the Jews accept it, word for word. Other religions try to change prior scripture, saying that it must have been poorly copied and misunderstood, or even deliberately altered to change its meaning – Islam and Mormonism both say this about the Bible. But we Christians accept the Tanakh exactly as it stands.

> *19 Whosoever therefore shall break one of these least commandments, and shall teach men so, he shall be called the least in the kingdom of heaven: but whosoever shall do and teach them, the same shall be called great in the kingdom of heaven.*
> *20 For I say unto you, That except your righteousness shall exceed the righteousness of the scribes and Pharisees, ye shall in no case enter into the kingdom of heaven.*

Here is another difficult passage: Jesus is saying that the Law of Moses is a true and correct indictment against us, and that unless we are completely righteous by that standard of that law, we cannot enter Heaven. Jesus has raised the bar from difficult – keeping the Mosaic law to the best of our ability, and then offering sacrifice for our failures – to an absolute impossibility: Keeping the law not only to the letter, but to the intent as well. In the following verses, Jesus teaches us how impossible it is to be righteous under the law.

This is to lay the foundation for what He will teach in later passages: That salvation does not come through the law, but through reliance upon His blood and His sacrifice.

You are invited – encouraged! – to read the remainder of the passage, which continues into the seventh chapter.

John 3:1-20

> *1 There was a man of the Pharisees, named Nicodemus, a ruler of the Jews:*
> *2 The same came to Jesus by night, and said unto him, "Rabbi, we know that thou art a teacher come*

> *from God: for no man can do these miracles that thou doest, except God be with him."*
> *3 Jesus answered and said unto him, "Verily, verily, I say unto thee, Except a man be born again, he cannot see the kingdom of God."*
> *4 Nicodemus saith unto him, "How can a man be born when he is old? Can he enter the second time into his mother's womb, and be born?"*

When Christians speak of being "Born Again," this is what they're talking about. Jesus is comparing becoming His follower to a metaphorical rebirth. Nicodemus, it seems, tries to understand this literally, but that's not what Jesus is telling him. Jesus explains it to him this way:

> *5 Jesus answered, "Verily, verily, I say unto thee, Except a man be born of water and [of] the Spirit, he cannot enter into the kingdom of God.*
> *6 That which is born of the flesh is flesh; and that which is born of the Spirit is spirit.*

There are different interpretations of "born of water and of the Spirit;" some take this to mean physical birth (referring to the water that precedes it) and then a second spiritual birth as we become Christians. Others take this to mean that at the moment of baptism ("born of water") we receive the indwelling Holy Spirit. In either case, we must have the second spiritual birth, that is, the moment of putting the past behind us and becoming a newborn creature in Christ. Compare 2 Corinthians 5:17.

> *7 Marvel not that I said unto thee, 'Ye must be born again.'*
> *8 The wind bloweth where it listeth, and thou hearest the sound thereof, but canst not tell whence it cometh, and whither it goeth: so is every one that is born of the Spirit."*

Spiritual things seem strange, even inscrutable, to the non-Christian. Remember to keep this in the right order: If something is from God, non-Christians will not fully understand it; but that does not mean that if people do not fully understand something, that it must therefore be from God. Be very careful with this.

> *9 Nicodemus answered and said unto him, "How can these things be?"*
> *10 Jesus answered and said unto him, "Art thou a master of Israel, and knowest not these things?*

Note that Nicodemus is one of the foremost scholars of his day, and a member of the Sanhedrin, a ruling body that is something like a civil grand jury today. But Jesus says that this scholar does not understand the basic ideas of Christianity, even though they are spelled out in the Jewish law. Again, Jesus is building a foundation for something else.

> *11 Verily, verily, I say unto thee, We speak that we do know, and testify that we have seen; and ye receive not our witness.*
> *12 If I have told you earthly things, and ye believe not, how shall ye believe, if I tell you of heavenly things?*
> *13 And no man hath ascended up to heaven, but he that came down from heaven, even the Son of man which is in heaven.*

And there it is. Jesus is speaking in the third person, calling Himself "the Son of man," but He expressly states that He has been to Heaven, and came down from Heaven to be there, in first-century Judea, speaking to Nicodemus. This is calling Himself God Incarnate. He is saying, "I came here from Heaven to be a witness to you of spiritual things you cannot yet understand."

> *14 And as Moses lifted up the serpent in the wilderness, even so must the Son of man be lifted up:*
> *15 That whosoever believeth in him should not perish, but have eternal life.*

See Numbers 21:5-9. Jesus is claiming that He will be "lifted up" as if on a pole, and that believing in Him will not merely save people from snakebite, but will give them eternal life. God saved the people in Numbers 21; Jesus will do the same when He is "lifted up." This equates Him with God – a bold claim that would be blasphemy if it were false.

> *16 For God so loved the world, that he gave his only begotten Son, that whosoever believeth in him should not perish, but have everlasting life.*
> *17 For God sent not his Son into the world to condemn the world; but that the world through him might be saved.*
> *18 He that believeth on him is not condemned: but he that believeth not is condemned already, because he hath not believed in the name of the only begotten Son of God.*

Take note here: Jesus' purpose was not to condemn the world; it was already condemned. Jesus' purpose was to save the world – that is, us – from our own failure. Again, Jesus is claiming to be God, and to be able to save us from sin.

> *19 And this is the condemnation, that light is come into the world, and men loved darkness rather than light, because their deeds were evil.*
> *20 For every one that doeth evil hateth the light, neither cometh to the light, lest his deeds should be reproved.*

The reader is invited and encouraged to read the rest of John chapter 3. It is a very enlightening chapter.

Note how this teaches the doctrines we discussed in Stage 0: We see from the sermon on the mount that the Mosaic Law is correct and true. We see that it is impossible to keep – we are sinners, and we can do nothing to save ourselves from sin. We see from the interview with Nicodemus that sin is deadly to our souls, but that God's gift, Jesus, makes it possible for us to be saved despite our sin. We must merely believe on Him.

An Elephant in the Room:

Let me say it clearly: when we talk about Christianity, there are many elephants that sneak into the room. At times, there are so many elephants that it's like a zoo, or possibly even a pachyderm convention. So let's address one of them now: Which Bible should I read?

You see, there are many versions of the Bible, many translations, many paraphrases, many editions, many revisions. Surely, since these are all different, one of them is the "right" Bible and the rest are wrong, right?

Unfortunately, it's not that simple.

The Bible was originally written in three languages. The Old Testament, or the Tanakh, was written primarily in Hebrew, with a little bit of Aramaic. The Aramaic is mainly found in parts of the book of Daniel. The New Testament was primarily written in a form of ancient Greek known as Koine Greek.

If you want precise accuracy in your Bible reading, then learn to read Hebrew and Koine Greek. If, on the other hand, you are willing to trust the Holy Spirit of God to help you to understand the Bible, then a modern English translation may better suit you.

The most respected English translation is the King James Version, or the Authorized Version. It was translated by a group of scholars commissioned by King James I of England – the fellow who was very nearly exploded by Guy Fawkes ("Remember, remember, the fifth of November").

Because James I commissioned the translation, it is referred to by his name. Because he authorized it to be made, and for ordinary Christians to read from it, it is called the "Authorised Version." Before that time, it was forbidden by English law to translate the Bible for general reading. Of course, we no longer need a King's authority in order to translate or to read the Bible, so the fact that it was authorized is no longer relevant to us in the church today.

I have had people tell me that King James changed the Bible, and that's why it has his name on it. That's absurd, of course; you can read from the same manuscripts that the King James' scholars used, and translate it for yourself. Let me know if you find any changes, won't you? King James commissioned the translation, and he was not personally involved with it beyond that point.

The problem with the King James Version, or KJV as it is commonly called, is that it was translated into 1611 English. It reads like Shakespeare, who was alive when the KJV was translated. It contains words we no longer use, such as "bewrayeth," and it contains constructions with deceptive meanings, such as "fetched a compass." We would take "fetched a compass" to mean that someone obtained a navigational device. In 1611, it meant that someone had turned completely around.

There were other (unauthorized) English translations at that time, such as the unauthorized Wycliffe and Tyndale versions, each of which obtained death sentences for the translators. Scholars and priests had access to a translation known as the Douay-Rheims, which is still preferred by some Roman Catholics, to this very day. These differ slightly from the KJV in the choices of words or the use of certain phrases, but they have the same meanings, and are useful for comparison. However, they also read as if they were written by Shakespeare.

They do serve the excellent purpose, however, of disproving the claim that King James wrote, altered, changed, or otherwise affected the meaning of the Bible as we have it. Compare, and see for yourself.

Because the KJV is difficult for modern readers, other English versions have been developed. The Revised Standard Version, or RSV, translated in the mid-1800s, was intended to correct some of the minor typographical errors of the KJV, but it is translated into the English of the mid-1800s. We no longer speak the way that Abraham Lincoln spoke, and thus the RSV is not ideal for us either.

In the 1970s, there was a tendency towards paraphrases, in which the writer does not refer to the original manuscripts, but simply changes the archaic words to modern words or phrases. Some people feel that this loses some of the meaning; others feel that the primary meaning comes through, and that secondary meanings can be learned later. The Living Bible is an example of a paraphrase. More recently, The Message paraphrase has gained popularity.

A group of scholars in the 1970s translated the New American Standard, or NASB, from the original manuscripts, using newer discoveries such as the Dead Sea Scrolls** to verify their content. NASB follows a word-for-word translation scheme, and produces a very literal translation, whereas the New International Version

(NIV) following a similar methodology but an idea-for-idea method, produces a more readable but less literal translation. In each case, there is a balance of reading ease versus scholarship.

We need to make a digression here to define our terms. First, when we speak of a manuscript, we do not mean that the author of the book touched that piece of paper (or papyrus, or parchment, as the case may be). We instead mean a hand-written copy of an earlier manuscript, itself a copy, dating back to the autograph. The autograph is the paper on which the original author wrote.

When we say that the translators of a given version used the original manuscripts, we mean that they used the manuscripts that we have, as we received them. Newer discoveries, such as the Dead Sea scrolls, add to our knowledge by giving us a comparison from an earlier point in history.

With the invention of the printing press, the copy-to-copy method has largely faded away. The modern impression is that it was like a game of Chinese whispers, or the telephone game, in which each player in a line whispers a phrase to the next player. When the last player says the received phrase aloud, it seldom matches the original phrase. Anti-theists in particular would have us believe that the Bible's original meaning has been lost over the ages through a haphazard method of copies.

The comparison to Chinese whispers is, of course, absurd. In the children's game, the whisper is an ephemeral communication that must be received precisely in the sole opportunity that a player is given to receive it. The original sound waves are lost immediately upon being spoken, and exist from then on solely in the mind of the hearer. But in the process of copying manuscripts, the original is not lost. The scribe is able to compare his work to the original, and to see if errors have been made.

In the ancient Hebrew tradition, three error-checks were made each time. The first consisted of a word count. If the new copy did not match the word count, it was immediately destroyed. This was followed by a letter count. Again, a mismatch would result in the destruction of the new copy. Finally, a comparison by reading was made. Another scribe would read the original aloud, and the scribe would follow along in his copy. Again, any error was cause for immediate destruction. We see a more modern process like this in the Herman Melville novel *Bartleby the Scrivener*.

Even after the copying, the originals are not lost. In time, of course, the eldest manuscript copies will fade, be destroyed, or wear into dust. But for many decades, or even centuries, they exist and are subject to verification through comparison.

That's not to say that no errors were ever transcribed. There are differences in the most ancient copies of some manuscripts, when compared with later ones. But the differences are minutia: The change of an article from "a" to "the," for example. There are studies elsewhere of manuscript differences, so we won't discuss them further here. Suffice it to say that we can have confidence in the manuscripts as we have received them in the 21st century.

Returning to Bible translations and versions, we can see that not all translations are the same. Clearly, a paraphrase, being one layer removed from the translation upon which it was based, will not have the same authority as a translation drawn from the best available manuscripts. Nonetheless, we must also consider the active agency of the Holy Spirit in the translation and in the reading of God's Word.

It is my belief that any translation which is made by sincere worshippers of the One True God, with the intention of glorifying Him and revealing His Word to those who have not heard it, will be augmented in both the translation and the later reading. How, you ask? By the Spirit of that same God, whose Word it is, and whose breath into human hearts inspired the original writing of it.

There are counterfeits, of course. Certain groups have undertaken to write their own Bibles, shaping their scholarship around their own doctrines. In one infamous example, known as the Joseph Smith Inspired Version, an American man claimed to be correcting errors (by divine revelation) that had been introduced into the Bible over the centuries. He went so far as to add chapters to the book of Genesis, in which he described himself, as if the original book of Genesis had prophesied that he would come to correct it. The JSIV is held to be scripture by a Missouri-based group known as the Community of Christ (Formerly the RLDS).

Another example of doctrinal twisting lies beneath the New World Translation, which the Jehovah's Witnesses wrote in order to support their more spurious doctrines. I would advise readers to avoid both the New World Translation and the JSIV. ***

But among translations made sincerely for the purpose of glorifying God, I recommend any translation that enables you to understand the Word of God. If you are not certain that the version you are reading is doctrinally sound, there are several things that you can do, such as comparing versions, discussing versions with other Christians, or praying that God will guide you to the translation He wishes for you to read.

Endnotes for Stage One:

* The gospel-writers state that Jesus made many statements. Critics challenge that some of these are duplications – Matthew appears to quote Mark, and Luke appears to quote both Matthew and Mark. Other critics assume the similarities to come from an as-yet-undiscovered document known as "Q." Q is alleged to be contemporary quotations recorded from various speeches and sermons of Jesus, and later cited by the gospel-writers. This would explain why all claim that Jesus said more or less the same statements, albeit in different contexts and different wordings.

Thus, in the view of those who favor a Q document, Jesus might not have made one single sermon on one single mount. Instead, perhaps Matthew concatenated a series of the Q citations into one single sermon that was typical of sermons Jesus preached.

The traditional view is that Jesus made many of these statements more than once, thus they may be heard in slightly different wordings and contexts without having to refer to a Q document. Matthew records them as he recalls them, perhaps refreshed by John Mark's gospel. Mark's gospel, in turn, is likely based on the recollections of Peter, for whom John Mark served as a scribe. Luke compiled all of the stories of Jesus that he could gather, and then placed them as nearly as possible into chronological order, using Matthew and Mark as guides, timelines, and sources.

We should also note that in the ancient world, the concept of plagiarism was unknown.

** The Dead Sea Scrolls, or DSS, were discovered in a cave at Qumran, in Jordan, in the year 1947. They were stored in that cave by a group of Jewish scholars – A socio-political party known as the Essenes – in about the year 70 AD (the time of the destruction of Jerusalem and of the second temple).

When these scrolls were analyzed, they were discovered to include many manuscripts of Bible books. For example, there was an almost-complete manuscript copy of the book of Isaiah, and it agrees perfectly with the received manuscripts as we have them today. Thus we have a first-century verification of the manuscripts that we have from, say, 300 or 400 AD.

It should be noted that there were also many mss. that had nothing at all to do with the Bible. Some of them might even have been original works by certain Essene scribes. If you can imagine that the local city library were to be buried, and rediscovered in the year 3996, you may see the magnitude of the problem. It would be a mistake for a 3996 AD archaeologist to discover an Isaac Asimov book in the *I, Robot* series, and to place it in the same context as the Encyclopedia Britannica, or even last year's phone book.

So on the one hand, DSS manuscripts of books of the Bible are valuable tools for comparison and for translation, but on the other, not every DSS book pertains to the Bible.

*** I would recommend one of three translations of the Bible for most new Christians and for those seeking to understand Christianity from the outside: The New International Version (NIV), the English Standard Version (ESV), or the Holman Standard Version (HSV).

Many of my Roman Catholic friends prefer the Douay-Rheims version, and I am told that The Message is also very good, but as I have not read very much from either, I hesitate to personally recommend them.

STAGE TWO
Sharing the Faith

I WAS RECENTLY teaching a class. I chose a member at random. I asked him, "Paul, if someone where you work were to say to you, 'I've seen that you are different, and I want what you have,' what would you say to lead that person to Christ?"

Before Paul could answer, a woman raised her hand. "Could he do that?" she asked. "He's not a minister or a priest or anything. Can he lead someone to Christ?"

The short answer is "Yes." Yes, you can show someone the path to faith in Jesus. You can't make them do it. You can't give them faith. You can't make the Holy Spirit impress upon them their need for Jesus. But you can show them the way.

The point of the question was to introduce the Romans Road, which we talked about earlier. What's wrong with people? Romans 3:23 tells us: We're sinners. What's the cure? Romans 6:23 tells us: God's gift of eternal life. Why would God give us so marvelous a gift? Romans 5:8 tells us: God loves us. How do we get the gift? Romans 10:9-10 tells us.

You can use that simple explanation to explain the gospel of Jesus to someone. If you can't remember it all, just memorize Romans 6:23, and talk about the difference between wages (which you've earned) and a gift (which you cannot earn).

But that's getting the cart before the horse. We can't share the gospel with people until they are willing to listen. The question, then, is how to get them to listen.

Jesus told his disciples that he would make them fishers of men, that is, they would metaphorically draw people to Christianity is the same ways that they had formerly drawn fish into their boats. Let's talk about that analogy for a moment.

There are many ways to fish. My father was fond of going onto a lake and lowering a single baited hook, then waiting until a fish took the bait. He used to talk about using a taut line when he was a boy. This is a technique of putting several baited hooks across a stream, and then checking them from time to time.

Some anglers take a single net and cast it over an area near them, then use the net to capture several fish at once. Others lower nets from boats, to surround a school of fish. This technique has been used to catch hundreds, even thousands, of fish at once.

I have heard of people using "fish traps" that are easy to swim into, but fish find it difficult to swim out. I have also been told of people who wade into ponds and feel along the bank for catfish dens. On finding one, they will stick a hand into it. When the catfish bites their hand, they will pull the hand and the fish out of the den and throw the fish onto the shore for others to catch.

That last technique seems a bit odd to me, but I have to say that there are many ways to catch fish. By analogy, there are many ways to prepare people so that they are willing to hear the gospel. Some of the fishing techniques consisted of one fisher looking for many fish. Others required several fishers for several fish. Your method of reaching people with the gospel may be one-on-one, one-to-many, or many-to-many.

Some of the methods require patience. Some require going away and letting the fish find its way in. Some of the methods are aggressive. Some of the methods allow the fish to come to the fisher; others require finding the fish where they live.

The analogy breaks down quickly: We are not fishing to harm the fish; we're not even trying to catch-and-release. We want to bring new believers to Christ, transform their lives, and then make them the same sort of fishers-for-humans that we have become.

Now let's take this idea out of the metaphor and put it into real life. There are many people in your life right now. Some of them have no interest in Christianity. Others are interested, but might be a bit skittish, perhaps because of bad experiences in the past or because they're afraid of getting pulled into something. A few people are very interested, but don't know who to ask. And a very few have no practical idea that Christianity is even an option for their lives.

Be aware of the people around you. Be aware of the conversations around you. You may feel a holy nudge to speak to someone, or to say that you are a believer. And that may be enough to turn a conversation towards the Romans Road. It may also have no effect at all, or none that you can see. It might even lead to a rebuke, or ridicule. If someone does make fun of you for saying something about your faith, remember Matthew 5:10 – 11, which was quoted after Stage 1: Be happy when you are cursed and made fun of for Jesus' sake. The prophets were treated the same way.

You may not be comfortable speaking to strangers, or even sharing your faith with friends. That's okay. There are other ways to share your faith. Even just living by moral principles will influence the people around you. Some of them will eventually ask you, in a setting where you do feel comfortable, why your faith makes you different.

There are other ways to share your faith. One way that seems to work well is to hold a party or a barbeque, and to invite your friends and neighbors. Arrange with your pastor in advance, or with the pastor and the deacons, so that they can be present and prepared. You can casually introduce them to your friends, and allow the subject to turn naturally to religion.

Because it is a casual environment, your friends and neighbors may feel more comfortable discussing spiritual things, and at the very least, they will see your pastor and your church as a comfortable, familiar group. Sometimes the road to the church is slow and gradual.

In 1922, a man named Arthur Flake published a book called *"Building a Standard Sunday School."* At that time, Sunday School was the primary outreach activity of most Protestant churches in North America, but his statements about Sunday School can be applied to any expansion of any church or ministry.

Flake created a formula of five points:

1. Discover the prospects.
2. Expand the organization.
3. Train the workers.
4. Provide the space.
5. Go after the people.

While not everything that the church would have done in 1922 will be effective in 2019, Flake's formula has been shown to be an effective tool for the church in nearly every instance.

Discovering the prospects – that is, finding people who are not involved in any church, and discovering how to communicate with them, is the first step. In 1922, this would have been accomplished by going door-to-door and asking if the residents attended a church. In 2019, it might be better done by sending emails, text messages, social media messages, and possibly even phone calls. *

Expanding the organization, in context of Sunday School, meant finding people to teach Sunday School classes. Today, depending on the context of your ministry, this might mean having greeters, ushers, worship leaders, and musicians. The important key here is that you need to have enough workers to help visitors fit into what's happening.

Training the workers is precisely what it sounds like. If you were creating a Sunday School, you'd teach the workers how to teach the Bible, and you'd provide appropriate tools and equipment – lessons, study guides, illustrations, graphics, and other collateral.

Providing the space is the next step, and often the most controversial detail. To grossly over-simplify the matter, you need meeting-places that are the right size, and neither too large nor too small. There should be enough room that everyone feels comfortable – not crowded or squished – but not so much room that everyone feels distant. As a general rule, our rooms are more likely to feel too crowded than not crowded enough.

Go after the people: You cannot have an effective ministry if it is a secret. In my experience, there are three mental stages through which a prospect must pass in order to commit to attending an event. First, he or she must know academically that the event will occur. Next, he or she must acknowledge that the event pertains to him or her, and finally, the person must make an act of volition – a conscious decision – to attend.

Suppose that you put up a flyer or perform a radio announcement that an event will be held on X date at X time. You may get a few attenders based on that simple information, but your return is likely to be very small – most people have only reached the first stage, which is a vague awareness of the event.

Now suppose that you are talking with a group of people, and someone asks about the event. You chat for a few minutes about the event, last year's event, and the details of what happens at such an event. Now, the people you're chatting with can see that the event pertains to them, and that it would not be impossible to attend. They can imagine what attending would require of them.

But if you were to turn to an individual, tell him or her about the event, with all of the details, and then conclude by asking, "Will I see you there?" you will have gone all the way to the third step. The person knows academically of the event; knows what the event is like; and is asked to choose whether or not to attend.

You will find that a direct personal invitation is far and away the best means for assuring good attendance at an event.

You can apply these principles to anything that your ministry does, whether it is a church service, a bake sale, a chili cook-off, a car show, or a Bible study. Flake's formula has proven very effective over time.

This can even be applied to your friends and coworkers. For your friends and coworkers to know that you attend church is usually not enough to encourage them to attend with you. Even if you talk about church on your work breaks, you're still only taking them to the second stage. But when you approach them one on one, and personally invite them to church, then you're likely to see good results.

This can backfire. I remember that once in the fifth grade, I asked a schoolmate if he wanted to go to Sunday School. He laughed in my face. Not everyone is open to the gospel. At the time, being laughed at by classmate was The End of The World. But I've come to understand, as you no doubt understand, that there will always be someone ready to laugh at us for something. Why then should someone's ridicule be a barrier to sharing the gospel?

We can't force a person to go to church, and if we did, the visitor would probably be more concerned with getting away from us than with anything the Spirit might say. We can only invite, but God must call and prepare the prospect.

End notes

---

* In the 20th and very early 21st centuries, there was a common device known as a telephone. From time to time, it would make an odd noise. When this happened, the user would hold it to his head and say "Hello."

Communications using such a device were known as "Phone calls." In the 20th century, these devices were at fixed locations, but by the 21st century, phones were mobile and could be found on the person of nearly everyone in North America.

Some Stage 2 Examples

One-on-one:

Acts 8:27-36 NASB
27 So he got up and went; and there was an Ethiopian eunuch, a court official of Candace, queen of the Ethiopians, who was in charge of all her treasure; and he had come to Jerusalem to worship,
28 and he was returning and sitting in his chariot, and was reading the prophet Isaiah.
29 Then the Spirit said to Philip, "Go up and join this chariot."
30 Philip ran up and heard him reading Isaiah the prophet, and said, "Do you understand what you are reading?"
31 And he said, "Well, how could I, unless someone guides me?" And he invited Philip to come up and sit with him.
32 Now the passage of Scripture which he was reading was this: "HE WAS LED AS A SHEEP TO SLAUGHTER; AND AS A LAMB BEFORE ITS SHEARER IS SILENT, SO HE DOES NOT OPEN HIS MOUTH.
33 "IN HUMILIATION HIS JUDGMENT WAS TAKEN AWAY; WHO WILL RELATE HIS GENERATION? FOR HIS LIFE IS REMOVED FROM THE EARTH."
34 The eunuch answered Philip and said, "Please tell me, of whom does the prophet say this? Of himself or of someone else?"
35 Then Philip opened his mouth, and beginning from this Scripture, he preached Jesus to him.
36 As they went along the road they came to some water; and the eunuch said, "Look! Water! What prevents me from being baptized?"

John 11:23-27 NASB
23 Jesus said to her, "Your brother will rise again."
24 Martha said to Him, "I know that he will rise again in the resurrection on the last day."
25 Jesus said to her, "I am the resurrection and the life; he who believes in Me will live even if he dies,
26 and everyone who lives and believes in Me will never die. Do you believe this?"
27 She said to Him, "Yes, Lord; I have believed that You are the Christ, the Son of God, even He who comes into the world."

One-to-many:

Act 10:44-48 NASB
44 While Peter was still speaking these words, the Holy Spirit fell upon all those who were listening to the message.
45 All the circumcised believers who came with Peter were amazed, because the gift of the Holy Spirit had been poured out on the Gentiles also.
46 For they were hearing them speaking with tongues and exalting God. Then Peter answered,
47 "Surely no one can refuse the water for these to be baptized who have received the Holy Spirit just as we did, can he?"
48 And he ordered them to be baptized in the name of Jesus Christ. Then they asked him to stay on for a few days.

Another Elephant:

As we said, elephants tend to creep into this room. Earlier in this chapter, we mentioned "your pastor" and "your church." Some of you, at this point, will be wondering exactly what church you should be attending, and what pastor you should be listening to. Well, as with the Bible question, there's not an easy answer.

There are roughly 55,000 various denominations of Christian faith. There are also a few sects (I will avoid the pejorative term, "cults") which use Christian terminology, but which bear little or no resemblance to the actual Christian faith. An example of such a faith might be Rastafarianism, which uses many terms that sound Christian – references to Zion, use of the word "Lord." It even bases itself in part on Abraham and Old Testament terms. However, it also contains many Hindu elements, and teaches the sacramental use of cannabis, along with strict dietary requirements. It teaches that Haile Selassie, an emperor of Ethiopia from 1930-1974, was the second coming of Jesus Christ,* which is contrary to the Christian teaching about the return of Christ.

Other non-Christian groups that are similar to Biblical Christianity are much more soothing to the ear. In discussing one group, I heard a woman say, "It all sounds very reasonable at first, and then, next thing you know, you're wearing magic underwear."

The best way to avoid being drawn into a pseudo-Christian faith is to know the Bible. We mentioned in stage 1 that it is important to read the Bible, to read it faithfully, and to pray about what you read. We mentioned that it is important to find a Bible that you can read carefully and prayerfully. Many of the letters in the New Testament, including the entire book of Galatians, include warnings about false teachers.

But even within Biblical Christianity, there are many denominations. There are the Roman Catholics, the Eastern Orthodox Catholics, the Protestants, and the Non-Conformists. Protestant denominations broke away from Roman Catholicism in the great reformation, over practices and doctrines that they felt were non-biblical. Some of the divisions were political – one would be hard-pressed to name a strong doctrinal difference between an Episcopalian and a Roman Catholic – and others were doctrinal, down to small details in many cases.

In general, Protestants divide into Arminian and Calvinist doctrinal positions. Arminians teach that we are saved by Free Will, that is, we choose of our own Free Will to accept the grace that God has offered through Christ. Calvinists, on the other hand, teach that God fore-ordained that certain people would believe, and those who are foreordained are drawn to God by Irresistible Grace. A strong case can be made for either side, and neither doctrinal group denies that the other is saved and will be in heaven.

Non-conformists – and there is some debate over whether this group is truly distinct from Protestants – claim never to have been a part of Roman Catholicism, and thus never to have "protested" and broken away. A case can be made that modern Baptists derive from early Anabaptists, who in turn derive from Piedmontese and other non-Catholic European believers, as one example. Baptists tend to be "Modified Arminian" in their doctrine. They acknowledge free will, but also embrace a doctrine known as the security of the believer, which is contrary to the full Arminian position.

Sounds like a mess, doesn't it? How can you possibly find the One True Church out of 55,000 denominations? Well, it turns out that you don't have to.

95% of all Christians believe 95% of the same things. All Christian churches teach the same central core of beliefs. The places where we differ are the periphery. Neither an Arminian nor a Calvinist will deny that Jesus died for our sins; where those two positions differ is in how exactly He did it.

I once conducted a small and unscientific survey of Christian lay-people. I asked for only persons who call themselves Christians – a very low bar to entry – and I asked only two questions: First, can you agree with the five points of Paul's doctrine, and second, can you agree with the Nicene Creed? About 80 people responded.

You remember the pre-Pauline doctrine that we discussed in Stage 0: That Jesus died for the sins of mankind, was buried, rose from the dead, was seen by many, and will return. These are listed in 1 Corinthians 15. Nearly everyone agreed with that. One person disagreed with a literal return of Jesus, and I suspect that he might have belonged to one of those pseudo-Christian sects that we mentioned, but we'll leave that alone for now.

The Nicene Creed goes like this:

We believe in one God, the Father Almighty, Maker of heaven and earth, and of all things visible and invisible.

And in one Lord Jesus Christ, the only-begotten Son of God, begotten of the Father before all worlds, Light of Light, very God of very God, begotten, not made, being of one substance with the Father; by whom all things were made; who for us men, and for our salvation, came down from heaven, and was incarnate by the Holy Ghost and of the Virgin Mary, and was made man;

He was crucified for us under Pontius Pilate, and suffered, and was buried, and the third day he rose again, according to the Scriptures, and ascended into heaven, and sitteth on the right hand of the Father; from thence he shall come again, with glory, to judge the quick and the dead.; whose kingdom shall have no end.

And in the Holy Ghost, the Lord and Giver of life, who proceedeth from the Father, who with the Father and the Son together is worshiped and glorified, who spake by the prophets. In one holy catholic and apostolic Church; we acknowledge one baptism for the remission of sins; we look for the resurrection of the dead, and the life of the world to come. Amen.

A few of those responding, despite my explanations, thought that the word "catholic" above (with a small c) referred to the Roman Catholic church, (with a large C). In this context, it means "all-encompassing" – that is, the Christian faith does not just apply to a certain region of the world, or to a certain level of our existence, but to all parts of everything. It is universal.

Even so, 90% of all respondents agreed with both statements; 95% agreed once the catholic/Catholic confusion was cleared up. Remember, these were lay-people, that is, the ordinary folks in the pews, and not pastors or theologians. Nonetheless, they agreed on all the essential points. Many denominations were represented, including one curmudgeon that I'm pretty sure was a Holy-Polarized-Contrarian (That's not a real denomination).

My point is this: find a church that teaches from the Bible, without adding other books. Find a church that agrees with the Bible (and doesn't try to shape the Bible into its teachings). Find a church where you feel that the Spirit of God can teach you from the Bible. Find a church where you can reasonably say, based on your study of the Bible, that the churches in the Bible are describing the kind of church that you go to. Those are the biggest points. If you discover down the road that the church you're attending is Calvinist, and you find yourself leaning towards Arminianism, you can always change churches.

Incidentally, one of the marks of a pseudo-Christian group is that they teach that they alone understand the Bible, or that they alone are going to heaven. I encourage you to avoid any church where you hear such a teaching: Anyone who has followed the Roman Road is on his way to heaven, and the Bible is shockingly simple to understand while shockingly profound in its meanings.

Personally, I embrace the Southern Baptist faith. It is not perfect, but I believe that it accurately reflects the kind of church that the New Testament describes, and I believe its teachings to be Biblical. If you need a starting place for your church life, the nearest Southern Baptist church would be a good place to start.

Wait; I think I see the trunk of another elephant: Do you need to go to church? Can't you get all of your religion done by yourself?

Well, the core disciplines of Christianity are Bible reading and prayer, which are personal interactions between you and God. But the Bible teaches clearly that we need to assemble together for many reasons. One good reason is so that older, mature Christians can guide and teach the younger, less mature Christians. I have often drawn my Bible Study teacher aside and asked him difficult questions. Once he explained predestination versus foreknowledge to me in terms of a highway, and I still remember his excellent response to that difficult distinction.

We also need to draw together for encouragement. Solomon remarks on this in Ecclesiastes 4:6 and 7:

> *Two is better than one, for they have a good return for their labor. For if the one falls, the other will lift him up, and if the other falls, the one. But woe to the one who falls when he is alone.*

Christians may be thought of as coals in a fire. So long as they are together, they will keep each other warm, but when they are dispersed, the fire will quickly go out – they cannot hold their heat when they are separated. Christians can also be thought of as soldiers in battle: When we remain with our unit, we can cover each other and protect each other. When we split up, we become vulnerable to the enemy.

In addition to those reasons, gathering together provides another opportunity for the Spirit of God to speak to our hearts. I have left many church services with a clear direction from God that I lacked when I went in. At times, pastors have spoken a message so clearly aimed at my circumstances that I wondered how they knew what to say to address me so precisely. Of course, it was not the pastor: It was the Spirit who used his words.

So, to summarize: Yes, you need to be in a church. Yes, you need a pastor. You need to pick your church and your pastor based on the Bible and on sound doctrine. I suggest a Southern Baptist church, but you may find another mainstream denomination to be a better fit for you.

End Notes:

* Some Rastafarians consider Selassie to have merely been a prophet; nonetheless, the religion is incompatible with Christian faith.

STAGE THREE
Expressing your Faith.

OKAY, THIS IS where we really get down to all the "Christiany" things, right? So we'll need a bumper sticker with an outline of a fish, and a HUGE Bible to carry (but never read), and a lemon tree so that we can always have a sour expression on our faces. Oh, and we'll need one of those huge crosses with the beads on them, so that everybody know we're REAL Christians.

Or... not...

So, there are important things about the Christian faith and there are a lot of things that have gotten dragged into the Christian faith by different people's interpretation of the Christian faith. Part of our job as Christians is to sort out the things that really should be expressions of our faith – such as good works, a powerful peace, love for our neighbors, and a heartfelt joy even when things are going wrong, from things that just get dragged along – such as bumper stickers and huge Bibles.

Don't get me wrong, there's nothing wrong with a huge Bible, or a big cross, or a bumper sticker. But those aren't what it's all about. Christianity is meant to be a life-changing experience. Expressing your faith should be a process of letting God work through your life.

Cool, but, um, how, exactly? Well, first, Bible-reading and prayer need to be part of your daily life. Yes, I know, we talked about those already – but really, those are more important than everything else.

Another expression of your faith will be the church in which you choose to participate. Notice that I didn't say, "attend." Church is not like going to a movie. It's not even like joining the PTA. Church is a support group. It's a twelve-step program for sinful people. In many ways, it is like a family. It's meant for you not to just attend, but to participate in.

That can mean joining a Bible study group. It can mean teaching a Bible study group. It can mean going on a retreat. It can mean organizing the food pantry. It can mean making a point of welcoming those around you. It might mean participating in the welcoming ministries, greeting people at the door. It can mean sharing your experience and expertise with the church as a whole.

Don't get me wrong. The church does not exist so that you'll keep yourself too busy to sin. It doesn't exist to make sure everybody can do good works. But a church works on volunteers sharing their talents in the church as an expression of their faith.

You may not be ready for that. Do not feel that you need to be busy doing church things from day one. Instead, take the time to see what the church does, and find ways that the church fits you and your talents. Find where God is working through the church, and when God prompts you, join Him in that work.

I mentioned, a moment ago, that the church is a little bit like a twelve-step program. We are all addicted to sin, you see. Even the most important teacher in the church is still a sin addict at heart. Even the late Billy Graham, though I admire how he did very well at keeping his addiction under control. Even Mother Teresa was a sinner. Everyone in the church is a sin addict.

Step one, as we talked about in stage zero, is to admit that we are sin addicts – sinners, who do bad things and hurt other people. Step two is to admit that we are powerless on our own to deal with our sin. Step three is to call upon a power greater than ourselves, that is, Jesus Christ, the Only High Power. And on through the steps we go, living each day for God, one day at a time.

We meet on Sundays, not just to sing songs, pray, and hear someone talk about God. We meet because we need our Christian family to surround us and to help us work through the steps of our sin addiction. They will pray with us when we fail, rejoice with us when we do well, and share their own experiences so that we can learn from each other.

The church can also be compared to a hospital, designed to treat the sickness of sin in our souls. We Baptists teach that salvation has three stages. We are saved from the penalty of sin when we are saved, from the power of sin slowly as we live the Christian life, and finally from the presence of sin when we go to be with God.

Our purpose as a church is to bring people through the treatment process. Jesus is the only One who can cure sin. Our jobs are to be the nurses, the orderlies, the Physician's assistants, the ambulance drivers, and the paramedics, the receptionists, the janitors. Our job is to find where He is working, and to join Him in His work.

It's a lot of pressure, right? What if I mess up? What if I let everyone down? What if people find out that I sin and that I have messed-up stuff going on in my life? What if...?

It doesn't need to be stressful. God is ultimately responsible for what He makes out of us. He is the One in charge, and all we need to do is to listen for His direction, and be willing to follow Him – to join Him in His work as He teaches us where and how He wants for us to follow Him. Listen to Him, through your Bible reading and prayer. See where He leads, and follow Him there.

Here's an important thing to remember: Expressions of our faith need to be organic. By that, we mean that they grow naturally out of having Christ in your life. Expressions of Christianity are not things that we do; they are things that we are.

We don't say to ourselves, "I haven't been Christian enough; I need to go pray," or "I can check off something on my Christian to-do list if I pray over my lunch." Instead, we naturally find ourselves conversing with God, which might happen to be while we're about to eat. We don't do good works because they'll get us closer to heaven; We do good works because we love God and express His love to others by doing good things for them. We find ourselves hungry for the Word of God because we need its encouragement and its power in our lives.

Good works are not the point of our Christian life; they are a by-product of knowing and loving God. If I love God, I will love what He loves. For example, I will love people whom He loves. I will be kind because He is kind, and has been kind to me. As I strive to be like Him, I will naturally start to take on His attributes, such as His kindness.

There is a passage in the book of James that many people find confusing. By the way, the book of James is near the back of the

New Testament, and was written by the "brother" of Jesus, that is, a natural son of Joseph and Mary. * The passage goes like this:

"18 But someone will say, 'You have faith, and I have works.' Show me your faith without your works, and I will show you my faith by my works."

What James is saying here (James 2:18, please read the entire passage from 2:14-2:26) is that faith needs to be expressed. A person of true faith will act upon that faith, and works – good deeds, peace, love, kindness – will naturally result from it. When James says in a later verse that *"Faith without works is dead,"* he is not telling us to do good works so we will have faith. He is not telling us to do good works to demonstrate our faith. He is telling us that a real faith will naturally result in real works.

If we truly believe that Jesus loved us and died for us – if we have real faith in that fact – then we will tend to act upon it. We might not be willing to die for someone else, but we will at least be willing to love other people in the way that Christ loved us. If we truly believe that Jesus is the Prince of Peace, we will want to be at peace with our neighbors.

If we believe that God will meet our daily needs, we will help to meet the daily needs of others. If we believe that Jesus made a sacrifice to love us, then we will be willing – no, we will find it a joy – to love others even when it costs us something.

That's a hard teaching. Take it slowly. Begin by trying to be a little more like Jesus each day. Begin by trying to apply the Bible to your life, which will naturally draw you into prayer, and then let God guide your choices as you go through your day.

Not every choice is a spiritual choice. It will be very rare that God will expect you to pray over whether to have your eggs over-easy or scrambled. The blue socks or the gray socks, well, I'm not sure God is that concerned about your choices in hosiery. But whether you smile at the bus driver, or whether you hold the door for the person behind you – those are real choices that really do matter.

And you're going to get some of them wrong. Yes, there is a real and powerful faith inside of you that can transform lives and light up dark places in our world. But there is also a sinful nature, a natural tendency to make the wrong choice. Prayer and the Bible will nurture that faith, and God can use them to make good works blossom in your life.

In Galatians 5:19-23, Paul talks about the fruit of the flesh (that is, the results of sin addiction), and about the fruit of the Spirit (the results of having God's Spirit directing our lives).

> *19 Now the deeds of the flesh are evident, which are: immorality, impurity, sensuality,*
> *20 idolatry, sorcery, enmities, strife, jealousy, outbursts of anger, disputes, dissensions, factions,*
> *21 envying, drunkenness, carousing, and things like these, of which I forewarn you, just as I have forewarned you, that those who practice such things will not inherit the kingdom of God.*
>
> *22 But the fruit of the Spirit is love, joy, peace, patience, kindness, goodness, faithfulness,*
> *23 gentleness, self-control; against such things there is no law. (NASB)*

Your life is much like a flower garden. Whether you end up with a yard full of flowers or of weeds depends on which plants you cull out, and which plants you water. The default is always weeds. If you do not tend to the development of your soul, weeds – poor choices, bad works – will always take control.

Which leads us to an important point: From the time that you began reading this book until now, you've probably failed at least once. So give it up, close this book... No, no, no, don't do that. Failing is a natural part of the Christian life. You will definitely fail. You will find yourself doing things that are simply not right, and you will find that you have no excuse.

The Apostle Paul put it this way:

> *14 For we know that the Law is spiritual, but I am of flesh, sold into bondage to sin.*

15 For what I am doing, I do not understand; for I am not practicing what I would like to do, but I am doing the very thing I hate. (Romans 7:14-15 NASB).

Notice here that Paul has two problems: He doesn't do what he knows he should and he also does things that he hates to do. Sins of omission (not doing good things) and sins of commission (doing bad things). It's almost as if Paul was addicted to sin. Oh, right. He was, just like the rest of us.

Maybe that's what he meant when he said, "I am of flesh, sold into bondage to sin." It looks like the apostle who wrote half of the New Testament by himself was also tempted to sin, just like we are, and had to work to overcome the power of sin, day by day, just as we do.

Does that mean that it's okay to sin? After all, Paul keeps talking about us being "Not under the law, but under grace." So can I just keep sinning? Doesn't that make just Jesus' sacrifice even bigger and more glorious, bringing more glory to God?

Let's see what Paul said about that.

1 What shall we say then? Are we to continue in sin so that grace may increase?
2 May it never be! How shall we who died to sin still live in it?
3 Or do you not know that all of us who have been baptized into Christ Jesus have been baptized into His death? (Romans 6:1-3 NASB)

I would take that as a resounding "No." Paul even goes so far, in Romans 6:7, as to say this:

7 for he who has died is freed from sin.
(Romans 6:7 NASB)

So Paul is saying that when Jesus died for us on the cross, the curse of Adam (addiction to sin) died at the same time. If we have been baptized into the body of Christ, we are part of a body which, having died, is freed from sin. We have that same power to overcome the power of sin — if we choose to use it.

In other words, as we become more like Jesus, sin has less and less of a hold on our lives. The key to overcoming sin is to be like Jesus as much as we can — to walk with God, to pray, to read our Bibles, and to meet with other Christians, so that we can help each other to be more Christ-like.

It seems daunting. It seems like too big of a task. It seems like we can't possibly make it. We're just too weak and too human, by ourselves, to do it.

And that leads to a sea-story. When I was a much younger man than I am now, I joined the navy. One of the things that I had never considered until I reached boot camp was this: What do sailors do when a ship catches fire?

On land, you evacuate. On the sea, there's nowhere to go. You have to put the fire out, no matter how big the fire is or how devastating it seems. I have to confess that it scared me. How was I going to put out an engine room fire, with burning lube oil spraying from broken flanges? Was it even possible for me to do that?

As it turns out, the navy had already done the thinking for me. What I was supposed to do was to meet with the repair team at repair locker #5, and to follow the direction of the leader. He would assign each person a role, and the entire team, working together, would accomplish the entire process.

One person would lay out fire hoses and connect them to the fire main. One person would take the nozzle of each hose. Others would take positions behind the person on the nozzle. In a careful and well-planned process, the two hoses — one creating a shield of low pressure fog, and the other providing a fire-quenching high-pressure stream, would approach the fire and suppress it.

If it were an oil fire, then instead of water, the hoses would spray a purple potassium powder, and cover it with film-forming foam. One person had a dual nozzle spraying the powder to interrupt the fire, and the foam to cover the oil. A second person had a hose with a fog nozzle, to keep them all cool; others held the hoses; another person was up at the tank, adding more solution to make more foam. It all worked together.

There was already a method; I didn't have to figure out how to do it. And there was already a team. I didn't have to put out the fire; I just had to fill my role on the team.

It is the same way in our Christian lives. I don't have to figure out how I'm going to overcome the power of sin in my life. I just have to follow the plan God has already laid out. And I don't have to do it alone; there is already a team of experienced sin-fighters who will join with me to defeat the sin in my life.

They will pray with me. They will show me passages in the Bible. They will teach me. They will share experiences that have taught them lessons. Slowly but surely, the power of sin will be overcome.

If you find that you've blown it, start over. Ask God to forgive your failures, and start again with your Christian walk, reading the Bible, praying, and meeting with other Christians. Trust God to forgive you and to do the rest. The apostle John said this about God:

If we confess our sins, he is faithful and just to forgive us our sins, and to cleanse us from all unrighteousness.
1 John 1:9 KJV

God doesn't forgive the way that other people forgive, keeping score in secret so that our sins can be thrown in our faces when we sin the next time. No, God forgives and forgets. He lets it go. Psalm 103:12 says it like this:

As far as the east is from the west,
So far has He removed our transgressions from us.
(Ps. 103:12 NASB)

You will never go so far east that you will begin to go west. There is a north pole, and there is a south pole, but there is no east pole or a west pole. God forgives us from sin, and takes it infinitely far away from us.

God will not remind us of our failures; He instead coaches us towards success. Remember something that we talked about in stage 1: God convicts us to correct us; the accuser condemns us to destroy us. God, through the Holy Spirit, convicts us of sin in order to help us make it right. And once we have made it right, He forgets that we ever sinned.

But this chapter is on the expression of our faith, right? So why are we talking about God's forgiveness – His Grace?

Well, remember that prayer that Jesus showed to the disciples? It had a phrase in it:

Forgive us our trespasses, as we forgive those who trespass against us.

Part of the expression of your Christian faith lies in how you react to people who do bad things to you. Jesus forgave you for much worse insults than anything anyone has ever said about you. Jesus forgave more horrible injuries than anyone has ever inflicted upon you. If Jesus forgave you, and if you are trying to be more like Jesus, then what should be your attitude towards those who hurt you? Jesus described it like this:

Matthew 18:24-33 (NLT):

In the process, one of his debtors was brought in who owed him millions of dollars.

He couldn't pay, so his master ordered that he be sold-- along with his wife, his children, and everything he owned--to pay the debt. But the man fell down before his master and begged him, "Please, be patient with me, and I will pay it all." Then his master was filled with pity for him, and he released him and forgave his debt.

But when the man left the king, he went to a fellow servant who owed him a few thousand dollars. He grabbed him by the throat and demanded instant payment. His fellow servant fell down before him and begged for a little more time. "Be patient with me, and I will pay it," he pleaded.

But his creditor wouldn't wait. He had the man arrested and put in prison until the debt could be paid in full. When some of the other servants saw this, they were very upset. They went to the king and told him everything that had happened.

Then the king called in the man he had forgiven and said, "You evil servant! I forgave you that tremendous debt because you pleaded with me. Shouldn't you have mercy on your fellow servant, just as I had mercy on you?"

Forgiveness is a Christian discipline. You cannot praise God in your heart while you are holding a grudge against someone. Instead, you need to let it go. In light of what Jesus forgave, aren't the insults we receive really kind of petty? That doesn't mean that you need to allow people to continue to hurt you. But it does mean that you can't dwell on past injuries.

Here is a very powerful tool to have in your Christian walk: When someone hurts you, pray this prayer:

"Lord God, I forgive _____ who hurt me by doing _____. I release any claims that I have before you for vengeance against them. On the last day, if you will hold them responsible for what they have done in this life, then so be it; but I ask you to hold them blameless for everything that they done to me."

That is a powerful prayer, because it will release you from the weight of your anger. You won't need to remember what they've done. You won't need to relive the injury and to fret about revenge. Just let it go. Not only will it make you feel better, it will also draw you closer to Jesus, who prayed on the cross for those who were crucifying Him.

So how do we express our Christian faith?

By reading the Bible, by praying, by attending church services, by participating in what's happening at church, by showing the fruit of the spirit, by starting over when we fail, and by forgiving people who really don't even deserve it – but then, we don't either, do we? Doing these things will show the world that we belong to God, and will please Him.

This might be a good time to read Galatians 5 and to think about the things growing in your soul. Do you find more things on the first list – the fruit of the flesh? Or do you find more things on the second list, the fruit of the Spirit?

Step by step, one day at a time, we grow closer to Jesus, and as we do, we find less room for the fruit of the flesh, and more room for the fruit of the Spirit. Pray that God will help you to live a life more pleasing to Him. Let the fruit of the Spirit grow naturally in your life.

End notes:

* There are doctrine issues that tie into whether James was a natural half-brother of Jesus or one of his "brethren" in a broader sense, i.e., a cousin or close relative. The word "brother" as used in the New Testament could be used either way. There are also references to another brother of Jesus, named Judas or Jude.

Certain denominations teach that Mary never consummated her marriage to Joseph. As a result, she would not have borne any other children. The brothers of Jesus referred to in the New Testament would have been cousins: brethren in the broader sense.

Other denominations make the assumption that Joseph and Mary were like any other married couple, and consummated their wedding promptly (though the scripture clearly states in Matthew 1:25 that the consummation did not happen before Jesus was born). Thus the brothers would be Jesus' actual brothers (half-brothers, that is, since Jesus' father was the Holy Spirit).

You may hear varied opinions regarding the size of Joseph and Mary's family. You may also hear varied opinions about the relative ages of Joseph and Mary, which in turn derive from this same question. The two prevailing theories are very different. The first is that Joseph was as young as Mary or nearly so. The second is that Joseph was much older and married Mary primarily to care for her and to provide for her own eventual old age (a Levitical marriage of sorts).

The important point is that Jesus had 2 nominal brothers, one of whom, James the Just,** wrote a book of the New Testament.

** James the Just should be clearly distinguished from James the greater and James the less. James the greater – possibly called the greater because he was older or larger – was the brother of the Apostle John, who was also called John the Elder. These two, together, were the James and John known as the Sons of Thunder (Boanerges). Their father was Zebedee.

James the Less is another disciple, usually identified as James, the son of Alphaeus. James the less is stated to have a brother named Joses, who might have been the Joseph Justin mentioned in Acts 1, or the Joses Barnabas mentioned in Acts 4 and ff., or both, or neither of them.

Another Pachyderm:

Don't I need to be self-righteous and sanctimonious and smug? No, you just need to be who God designed you to be. Many people, especially people who write TV shows and movies, seem to feel that Christians are judgmental and hypocritical. Well, some are; we're all sinners saved by God's grace, and for some folks, sanctimonious self-righteousness is the sin from which they are being cured.

But in fact, Jesus gives us the power to be who we're supposed to be, without being judged by anyone. And if He has given us that power, shouldn't we share it?

But don't I have to, you know, hate gay people or something? No. God doesn't tell us to hate anyone. Again, we're all sinners, and we're all being saved from something. God loves everyone, and tells us to love everyone in His name. When Jesus taught us to love our neighbors as much as we love ourselves, he then expanded the meaning of neighbors to include everyone.

In fact, as Christians we are forbidden to have enemies. Jesus tells us to love our enemies and to pray for those who would "despitefully use" us (in other words, treat us badly). Every person we encounter, however rude, hateful, and odious that person may be, is still a person for whom Christ died. Yes, even THAT guy. Even THAT woman.

Yes, that person is evil (aren't we all?). Still, Jesus died for that person. And if He could love that person enough to go through crucifixion, can't we show them a bit of compassion as well? Even for Jesus' sake, as He would do in our place? Can't we pray for that person, and beg God that He might have mercy upon them?

Should I go stand on a street corner and wave a Bible and shout at cars? Well, is that where God is working? Is that where He's calling you to join Him, and to work with Him? Personally, I don't think it is, because I'm not so sure that it's effective. I've never met anyone who was saved because they drove by a corner where someone shouted at their car and waved a Bible at them. But ultimately, how you serve God is between you and the Holy Spirit. Read the Bible, pray, and ask God to show you where He is at work.

Okay, when people at work are doing stuff they shouldn't, I have to tell them that they're dirty rotten sinners, right? No. Let's be honest here: People know right from wrong. People know that they shouldn't gossip, or use vulgarities, or steal from the company, or whatever they're doing. You don't need to tell them that it's wrong; they already know that. Don't participate, and they'll gradually come under conviction without you needing to say a word.

People notice that I don't use certain words and phrases. If they use those around me, they usually apologize, even though I'm not offended. In fact, I was once a sailor – I've heard far worse. But the fact that I try not to do the wrong things sets an example for them, without me ever saying a word. I never need to tell anyone that he or she is a dirty rotten sinner.

It would be hypocritical anyway, since I'm a dirty rotten sinner myself, right?

Do I really have to forgive people? Don't you know what they did? They don't deserve to be forgiven! Jesus forgave us when we didn't deserve to be forgiven. If he can do that, can't we let go of a few things? Jesus told a parable about two servants… Oh, right, we talked about that a couple of pages ago.

Look, when you hold a grudge, or remember something that someone said to you, it is like holding onto a burning stick. You are the one who keeps getting burned, and who has to keep finding a way to keep the burning stick from setting fire to everything around you. That's a lot of work, and what good does it do you?

I know a man who has anger issues. From time to time, he will decide that someone has wronged him, and all that he talks about for that week will be how he feels that he was abused. Usually, the offender is one of his friends, and the insult may be so small that objectively, it seems like nothing unusual.

But to him, for that week, it will be the most important matter. And after a week or so, he gets over it. Months later, the pattern repeats. So he keeps burning his own fingers by holding onto his red-hot anger.

The problem is that it takes a lot of patience to be friends with a man who regularly accuses you of taking advantage of him. I have had to sit down with this friend and to say to him, "Look, here is the benefit that we each have from our friendship. See the balance. On the whole, we've each done good things for the other."

His anger keeps setting fire to the world around him. If he were able to let that anger go, and to release it – to say to himself that what others do to him is really not that important – he would be healed of many of his issues, just that quickly. But he won't.

There's another lesson in this also: on the one hand, I have to forgive continually him for thinking that I'm not a very good friend (I like to think that I'm an excellent friend). On the other hand, he has to forgive me for whatever slight he feels against me that week.

And while it's not as good as simply not allowing himself to feel angry, a system of constant forgiveness is the second best.

The Christian church is like that. The entire church consists of people who have to forgive each other all the time. There's that lady who sings too loud and off-key. There's that guy who laughs too loud, and at the wrong times. There's that brother who just never stops talking. But because we love them – and because we love them because Christ loved us – we forgive them. And they forgive us. Continually.

And here's the really sneaky thing about forgiving other people: There's nothing they can do about it. No one can force you to hate him. No one can make you be angry with him, or hold a grudge against him. You have the power to forgive.

But that's not how I see Christians behave on TV. I saw this one movie, and this guy used to ... Well, hopefully I don't have to explain that TV and movies are not reality, and most of the time aren't even a good reflection of reality. The fact is that Christians in media are usually portrayed very poorly. We're usually shown either as sour sanctimonious skunks or as greedy self-centered drunks.

Sadly, there are actual people who profess to be real Christians but who demonstrate absolutely no Christian love, justice, humility, or any mercy in their lives. I hate to admit it, but it's not completely wrong to paint Christians as self-centered – some of us are. Did I mention that we're all dirty rotten sinners?

But that's not what Christianity is about. Christianity is about our relationship with God, which expresses itself in our lives with love for others, forgiveness, peace, and mercy... Well, that entire "Fruit of the Spirit" thing from Galatians 5:22-23.

A Stage 3 Christian:

There was a man in a church, long ago and far away. His name was Joses, and to be honest, I'm not sure if it was pronounced like "Hoses" or like "Ho-Say" or like "Joe-Says" or like "Frank." Okay, I'm pretty sure he didn't say it, "Frank." I saw someone write his name as Joseph, so I'd probably call him Joe if I knew him.

There's a rumor that he was passed over for a big position of authority in his local church, but most folks think that was a different guy, named Joseph or Justin. If that really was Joses, then it just makes his attitude even greater.

Anyway, in the country where he lived, when he was there, it was very unpopular to be a Christian. You could be fired from your job, and no one would hire you after that. You could be put in prison, or even killed by mobs in the street. Your family wasn't safe, and sometimes your own family would throw you out on the street. People got divorces because one partner became a Christian. People were disowned. People got killed over it. It was a dangerous time and place to be a Christian.

Joses saw this. He owned some land, so he sold it and he brought the money to the church leaders, telling them to use it to feed the poor believers, who had lost everything for Jesus. He didn't brag, but word got around, and other Christians who had valuables began to sell them, just as Joses had done. That's one part of Joses' Christian example: He didn't brag about things he did, because he did them out of love, not so that people would think he was a great guy.

As I mentioned, this was a dangerous place to be a Christian. There was a teenager who hung around by the church, always trying to stir up trouble. His family was well connected, and knew all the politicians. He managed to get a lot of church leaders thrown in prison or killed. There was one murder on a public street – a church leader was surrounded and lynched by a mob because he spoke to them about Jesus. This young man was there, at the murder scene, an accomplice to the crime.

Well, one day this young man showed up and told the church leaders that he had changed – that he had met Jesus, and that he wanted to join the church. It was difficult to trust him, and all the church leaders thought he was up to some trick. All except one.

Joses believed him. Joses made it his personal mission to teach this young man and to vouch for him with the church leaders. In time, the young man became a trusted member of the church, but he eventually moved away.

Years later, the church sent Joses to do something important for them. Joses agreed, but first he went and found the dangerous young man, and brought him along. He mentored the young man, and eventually they began going on mission trips together.

Eventually, the young man excelled beyond his teacher, and became a respected church planter. Some teachers would have resented having a student become the teacher, but Joses gladly gave way, and let the younger man lead them.

Some of this may sound familiar to you, and if so, I'm glad. You can read of Joses in the Acts of the Apostles, where he is more often known as Barnabas, the son of encouragement. The young man he mentored was the Apostle Paul, who wrote about half of the New Testament.

The church to which Barnabas gave his gift was the church at Jerusalem, in around 36 AD, give or take a couple of years. I personally suspect that he was that Joseph, surnamed Justin, who was nominated as an apostle (except that the lot fell to another man, Matthias).

In any case, we see in Joses Barnabas a Stage 3 Christian, who lived what he believed, and who sacrificed for his brethren, not because he had to, but because of Christ in him. He did not put himself first, but allowed others to excel, and supported them in their work. He was unafraid to receive new Christians, and he taught them what he himself had been taught. This is what Christian maturity looks like:

1. Joses supported his church and his church leaders.
2. Joses gave quietly to feed the hungry Christian brethren around him.
3. Joses looked for the best in people, even if he had good reason to hate them or to fear them.
4. Joses made it his goal to mentor younger Christians.
5. Joses didn't insist on being the leader. He was willing to take a back seat when a student became the teacher.

6. Joses had such a positive and uplifting joy about him in all that he said and did that his friends called him "The Son of Encouragement."

If we believe (as I strongly suspect) that the Joses (Joseph) called Barnabas in Acts 4:36 was the same person as Joseph Barsabbas surnamed Justin in Acts 1:23, then we should add another characteristic:

0. Joses didn't let disappointment, or being overlooked as a leader, keep him from serving God and serving his church.

This is what it looks like to live what you believe. This is what it looks like to live the Christian faith. Can you be called a son of Encouragement by those around you? Do you lift others up and help them to find hope and joy, even in difficult times? Do you keep on working, even when you are passed over for promotions? Do the poor eat bread from your table?

Do you look for the good in people? Do you mentor younger Christians, and help them to avoid the pitfalls that have slowed you down? Do you let others take the glory, and allow others to lead?

In Stage 0, we talked about Micah 6:8, and the three things that God requires: Doing justice, loving mercy, and walking humbly before God.

Barnabas' gifts for the poor and his willingness to trust Paul show his love for mercy. Barnabas' willingness to work when he had been overlooked for a high position, his treatment of Paul as Paul matured in the Lord, and his overwhelming joy show his humility before God.

Some people feel that Barnabas was the writer of Hebrews, a major book in the New Testament. The author of Hebrews wrote powerfully, and produced the single most encouraging book in the entire Bible.

Can you become a Son or Daughter of Encouragement?

STAGE FOUR
What is Faith, anyway?

WE CHRISTIANS SPEND a lot of time talking about Faith. It's not a word that we hear very much outside of church. So what is faith, exactly? Is it how people get healed on TV (except for the people who don't have enough of it)? Is it just a holy word that means we wish for something?

The writer of Hebrews (many people think it was Paul, but I lean towards Barnabas) tells us that

Now faith is the substance of things hoped for, and the evidence of things not seen. By it, the elders gained a good report.   (Hebrews 11:1-2 KJV)

Now faith is confidence in what we hope for, and assurance about what we do not see. This is what the ancients were commended for. (Hebrews 11:1-2 NIV)

Confidence in what we hope for. Well, so if we wish for something really, really hard... No, that's not it. Hope is a reasonable expectation of a positive future event. I wish I could recall who it was who said that, and I hope that it will come back to me one day, but in any case, it is the best definition of hope that I have ever seen.

So faith is confidence in, or the substance of, something good that we reasonably expect in the future. Substance, by the way, comes from two Greek words, *sub* (beneath) + *stare* (to lie). Substance is that which lies beneath. We may have carpet on our floors, but the wooden boards are the substance that supports the carpet; they lie beneath and hold it up.

We as Christians have a hope of many good things to come: Life with God when this life is through; To meet Jesus face-to-face; To see our loved ones in Heaven. Our faith in Jesus underlies these, and gives us confidence in them. These are not things we wish for: These are things that, because of Christ, we reasonably expect.

It should be clear at this point that I can have faith in many things. When I cross a bridge, I walk in confidence because I have faith in the bridge and in the people who built it, that they knew what they were doing and understood the distribution of weight.

When I sit in a chair, I have faith in that chair. I have confidence in what I hope for (that it will hold me up) and assurance of what I do not see (the strength of the chair). It is the substance of what I hope for, it lies beneath my bottom and just as I hope, prevents my bottom from falling to the floor.

To digress for a moment: Remember what we said earlier, quoting James, that *Faith without Works is Dead*. I can believe that a bridge, or a chair, or a friend will support me. But until I act upon that belief, by crossing the bridge, by sitting on the chair, or by calling upon the friend in my time of need, my belief does me no good at all.

My faith may be well placed; the chair or the bridge may hold up perfectly beneath my weight. Or the bridge may give out, dumping me into a river. The chair may give out, dumping me into the floor. I may have faith that a friend will give me a ride home from work, but he may get lost, have a flat, or simply refuse.

This raises two important things about faith: First, my faith in the bridge or in the chair does not keep either one of them from collapsing, to my harm. My faith in a friend will not cause him to be faithful. Unfortunately, that's how many people understand faith; as a kind of magic pixie dust that makes miracles happen.

Faith is only as good as the object of the faith. My faith in God is not qualitatively different from my faith in a bridge, a chair, or a friend. But it is quantitatively different. God has infinitely more strength than any chair or bridge; He is infinitely more faithful than any friend.

This leads to another use of faith: We call someone "faithful" when that person lives up to our faith. If I expect a friend to give me a ride home, and he's waiting when I come out of work, he is faithful. In Revelation 19:11, John calls Jesus "Faithful and True."

These two words are somewhat redundant, which is good, because that lets us see the meaning of "Faithful" as reflected in the word "True." As John uses it in referring to Jesus, "True" means straight or consistent with something else. For example, if we say that someone is "True to his word" we mean that he keeps his word, and what he does is consistent with his word. If we say that something happens "True to form," then we mean that it happened consistently with the way it always happens.

If "True" means a consistency with what is expected, then "Faithful" as a partner to "True" must mean that Jesus is consistent with the faith we place in Him. He keeps His word; He acts consistently with His love; He lives up to His promises. He is faithful and true.

When we talk about the Christian Faith, we mean those things that we all, collectively, trust Jesus to fulfill. We trust Him to forgive our sins. We trust Him to place the indwelling Spirit within us. We trust Him to help us overcome the power the sin in our daily lives. We trust Him to raise us from the grave on the Last Day.

That's what we mean by the Christian Faith. It's very simple.

But you're thinking that it's not that simple, aren't you?

You probably read a book where people were talking about complicated Christian things. Like that Diet of Worms thing, and vows of poverty, and fasting. What about that book where that guy ran all over Rome looking at statues till he figured out who killed the Pope (or something like that)? Isn't that "The Christian Faith?"

Good questions, and very fair. Christianity has a long history – about 2,000 years – and not all of it reflects favorably on the Church. The church is full of sinners. In fact, everyone in the church, everyone who's ever attended a church, and everyone who has ever thought of attending a church – they're all sinners. Every single one of them. Of us.

The Diet of Worms was an important event – Diet means a certain type of religious meeting, something like a council, and Worms is a city in Germany where that Diet was held in 1521. It has nothing to do with fish bait, bird food, or anything like that. The principal topic of discussion was the Protestant Reformation. Do you need to know that to be a Christian? No. Not at all. Church history is interesting, but it's not the main point.

Over the ages, many devout Christians have taken various kinds of vows to God. One type of vow is a vow of poverty. St. Francis of Assisi was best known for his poverty: One historian remarked that St. Francis simply thought it impolite for him to be richer than any man to whom he was speaking.

A more modern example was Rich Mullins, whose songwriting and singing had a profound effect on modern Christian music. The proceeds of his music were directed into a trust that supported several charities. The directors of his trust were to pay Mullins no more than the average wages of a working-class individual, so that he would not be tempted to excess.

Do you need to take a vow of poverty? Probably not, but if you feel that wealth is creating a barrier between you and God, have a chat with your pastor and with respected Godly friends. Then make a decision based on what you feel that God is directing you to do. Vows are a useful tool for Christians — they are designed to remove stumbling blocks that might interfere in our relationship with God. But they are not the main thing.

Fasting is a Christian discipline that works with prayer to help us overcome distractions caused by our flesh. We might fast from a certain savory food during the time before Easter, so that we will have a reminder to pray and to wait for God. We might fast from sweet things, or even meat, for a few weeks, while we concentrate on a spiritual struggle.

In a few cases, where we feel a special need to keep our minds on prayer, we might abstain from all food (but not water) for as long as a day or two, praying whenever we feel hungry or weak. Any such total fasts should only be done by those healthy enough to do so, and those with any physical conditions should see a doctor before beginning a fast.

Again, it can be a useful tool for a Christian. But fasting is not what the Christian life is all about. Many devout Christians never fast, or fast very seldom. It's useful, but not the main point.

In all of these things, it is vital to separate the intrinsic from the arbitrary. Intrinsic things are the things that are necessary, vital, and part of the core of something. Arbitrary things are just an additional part.

On a car, the engine is intrinsic; the radio is arbitrary. The wheels are intrinsic; the hubcaps are arbitrary. The windshield is intrinsic; the color of paint is arbitrary. Some of the things have to be there – they are intrinsic. Other things are arbitrary.

For example, praying is intrinsic. Praying on your knees, with eyes closed and hands folded, is great – but it's arbitrary. You can pray sitting in a chair, standing on a flagpole, or driving a car. That you pray and talk with God – that's a key element of Christianity. How you do it is just how you do it.

What are the intrinsic elements of the Christian faith? Well, the intrinsic doctrines are that Jesus Christ died for the sins of humans, was buried, rose on the third day, was seen by many, and will return. The intrinsic practices are prayer, reading the Bible, and meeting with other Christians regularly. Everything else… Well, it may be important, but when you come down to it, it's arbitrary.

You can go to church in a storefront, in someone's barn, in a small country building, in a huge city building, in a cathedral, or in a warehouse. I've been to church meetings in all of the above except a barn. The intrinsic part was that there were church meetings, not where they were held. There might be candles on the altar, or no candles. There can be incense, or no incense. There can be a long sermon or a short one. There can be pews and hymnals, or chairs and song-sheets, or we can stand and sing from memory.

Anything that is not intrinsic can be done as the Spirit leads.

We do need to be careful that we conduct our meetings (and ourselves) in a way that glorifies God. We can't rob banks in the name of God, because that violates His principles. We can't do evil in the name of Good. We need to remember that the things of God are sacred, and that they belong to Him.

We can worship in many different styles, but the style needs to be Godly and pleasing to Him. We can pray as the Spirit leads us, but we need to remember that we're talking to God. We can read the Bible anywhere, any time, but we can't mock the Bible and make fun of it. It is the sacred Word of God and an important part of our faith.

But within those guidelines, that we worship God is more important than how we worship God; our faith is more important than how we express our faith.

In the next chapter, we will talk more about the practice of our faith through church services.

A Completely Tangential and Pointless Digression:

While we're talking about Christian History, we should mention the Defenestration of Prague. We talked about it in Stage Zero, and mentioned that we'd get back to it. Well, we're back.

The Defenestration(s) of Prague were two events where some folks got thrown out of some windows. As much as I hate to admit it, there have been some times in Church History where Christians didn't really treat other Christians very well.

The area around Prague, which is now known as the Czech Republic (even Czechs reject the name Czechia), was a mostly Roman Catholic area, but was ruled by Protestants. This was during a time when each of those groups considered the other corrupt and heretical. We've learned to get along better since then. By the way, did I mention that we Christians are all dirty rotten sinners, who happened to have been saved by God's merciful grace?

So, in each of these events, the Protestant authorities came to Prague to impose strict rules and restrictions on the Catholics. While they were announcing this policy to the Catholics, the Catholics became so enraged that they rushed the Protestant leaders, seized them, and threw them out the open second-floor windows. No one was seriously injured, because there happened to be wagons full of dung outside the window, which broke their fall.

What truly amazes me about the Defenestration of Prague is that it happened twice. You'd think that the Protestant leaders, walking into the building a second time, would have said to themselves, "Hey, remember the last time we were here? Aren't those the same dung-wagons? Should we maybe try meeting on the ground floor this time?"

So, what lesson about Christian behavior can we learn from the Defenestration of Prague? Well, none that I can think of, unless it's to be nice to your fellow Christians, especially when you're on the second floor and don't like the smell of what's parked outside.

We can find many examples of people throughout Christian History getting it completely wrong, as here: The Protestants lording over the Catholics, and the Catholics reacting quite angrily. Imagine if the Protestants had instead been gracious – treating the Catholics with Justice (Micah 6:8, anyone?) and the Catholics had reacted with Mercy (Micah 6:8, anyone?) and they had all walked humbly before God (As in, say, Micah 6:8)?

Well, that would have been a completely different kind of an event, wouldn't it? We might have referred to it as the Great Reconciliation of Prague, and everyone might have wound up smelling like roses… instead of… Well, not-roses.

Just a thought. We now return to the prior discussion.

STAGE FIVE
Practicing the Faith.

THERE IS A STRANGE thing that happens as you start spending time in church: You begin to become the church. You don't become a building, with a belfry on top, but that's not what a church is. The church is the people. The building where they meet is merely that: a church building.

As you become a part of the church – that is, as you take part in the things that the church does – you will find yourself taking on different roles in the church. If you study the Word for a while, and spend time in Bible studies, you might be asked to lead a Bible study. If you spend a lot of time at prayer meetings, you might be asked to lead in prayer, or even to lead the meeting. Yes, Christians do meet just for the purpose of praying together. Often on Wednesday nights.

As you gradually grow in the Christian faith – which means learning more about the Bible through reading and study, and learning more about God by spending time with Him in prayer – you will be drawn into deeper and deeper roles of service. At some point, you might even need to organize a church meeting of some sort.

Not everyone will be asked to lead in the church. Not everyone is shaped for being a leader. The Apostle Paul talked about how God gives different gifts and different roles to various people. I know one young man in our praise team who can play the guitar beautifully, but if he were asked to speak, he would be utterly terrified. I know other people who cannot stop talking. I know one elderly lady who is unbelievably wise: She always seems to know what to say in every situation.

Whether God has given you gifts, skills, and experiences that enable you to lead, or to advise, or to follow, or to fill any of a thousand roles in the church, it will be helpful to know how church services are organized. Most church services follow a simple pattern. In this chapter, we will be talking about what church services are like.

Please keep in mind that in the discussion below we are talking about current Christian traditions and practices. The Bible does not tell us what a church service should look like. Well, it gives us guidelines, such as that we should be orderly in our worship, and it says that we need to treat everyone in the service with equal dignity. It says that the early believers sang songs, praised God, and read the Bible. It says that preachers spoke to people about the meaning of the scriptures. It says that they met to worship and to pray in houses, and in the temple (while the temple was still there).

The Bible doesn't say to pray this many prayers, sing that many songs, and preach for this many minutes. All of the procedures that follow are merely traditions, handed down to us by humans from other humans before them.

Not all church services are anything like what is described here, and not all church services should be. These are offered to you as examples, and not as templates. In the end, the Holy Spirit of God will be your ultimate guide to how to worship.

With that in mind, let's suppose that you find yourself with a group of believers and wish to hold a worship service, but don't know how. Here is an example of a how a Sunday worship service might be arranged.

In general, there are three parts: The song service, the sermon, and the benediction. We sing praise to God, we listen to a message from God's word, and we are blessed. Each of these parts has smaller parts within it.

The song service will usually begin with a Call to Worship. This can be a song, a prayer, or someone up front saying, "Everyone listen up, we're going to sing now." The purpose of the call to worship is to give the service a clear and definite beginning.

The first song is usually called an invocation. It invokes, or calls down, the presence of God, and asks His blessing on the service. There may or may not be an invocation prayer right after the invocation song.

In general, the invocation will be a strong, loud, and powerful song. If your church is the hymns and hymnal type, the invocation might be "Holy, Holy, Holy" or "A Mighty Fortress" or something along those lines. If your church is more contemporary, the invocation might be something like Matt Redman's "Ten Thousand Reasons." Of course, in a few years that will be an "old" song, and the popular invocation might be something we can't yet imagine.

The invocation prayer, if there is one, should be specifically about asking God to be present and to bless the service. We already know that Jesus will be present in the service; this is a given. He Himself said that where two or more gather in His name, He will be in their midst. The Holy Spirit indwells each Christian, so where Christians gather, the Spirit of God is present. In this way, the invocation is really not necessary, except as it formally recognizes God's presence, and dedicates the service to His glory.

The second song is usually a hymn or song of praise. It is meant to recognize and to call out the goodness and glory of God, and the complete work of Jesus for our salvation. It is a declaration of our awe before God. It is a key element in focusing the worship on a specific theme.

There may be an offering taken at this point. Ah, see, you knew that money would come into this somewhere, right? Well, frankly, someone's got to pay the electric bill and put tissue boxes on the altar. But the offering is not about paying the bills so much as it is about giving the believer a chance to put God ahead of our finances. In giving, we recognize that all we have is a gift from God.

Visitors are usually instructed not to give, and the service leader will usually say something to that effect. No one should feel that he or she must pay to come to church. The offering is an opportunity, and whether you give nothing, a little, or a lot is a matter between you and God.

Jesus even remarked on offerings once. He pointed out that the rich were giving big offerings, casting their coins into the chute so that the coins would rattle and make a lot of noise, calling attention to the size of the gift. But a widow quietly slipped up to the offering chute and secretly slid a tiny coin into the collection. Jesus told his disciples that the widow had done more than the rich men, because while they gave excess from their wealth, she was cutting deep into her budget to give that tiny coin. And she did it secretly, knowing God would take care of her.

So, in short, don't obsess over the offering.

The third, and usually final song, is generally in a slower tempo, and is intended to focus our minds on our response to God's goodness and what Christ did for us on the cross. We want to prepare for the sermon, and to compose our minds to more serious consideration of God.

We generally close the song service with a brief prayer, which also asks God to bless the speaker and his message.

The sermon is fairly self-explanatory. It is a discussion about God, based on His Word, and it is intended to teach us, to speak to us, and to lead us deeper into the Christian life. Usually, a pastor will read a scripture. Then he will talk about that scripture, explaining what it means, and then explaining how to apply it into our lives.

An easy mnemonic for remembering the structure of a sermon might be hook, look, and took. First, there should be a point that makes us think, and that draws our attention to the passage. This is the hook. The second part examines the passage and gives us something to consider. This is the look. Finally, the sermon should give us homework – something to take away from the sermon, and apply in our daily lives. This is the "took" (the part we take away).

In another generation, long, long ago, people sometimes referred to a sermon as "three points and a poem," and that's not a bad framework for a sermon, even today. A sermon should not be too brief, or the listeners will not have time to think through what the scripture is telling them. On the other hand, it must not be too long, or the earliest parts will be forgotten by the time the speaker finishes.

There are some sermon styles that should be avoided. One of these is the classic "Tell them what you're going to tell them, then tell it to them, then tell them what you told them." While there was a day when an hour-long sermon was standard fare, it is no longer an effective method in today's culture.

Sermons need to have a focus. In the last few months, I have heard sermons that were tightly focussed and had a solid impact, and sermons that were loosely focussed and gave a good general nudge to the listeners.

I have also heard a speaker whose sermons were like laser beams. I would sit in the congregation and look around nervously, because I suspected that everyone knew he was speaking about me. As it turns out, the pastor didn't know me, but the Holy Spirit was able to take his words and to highlight things wrong in my life; things that I needed to change.

Not every pastor will have that focus. We are not all given the same gifts. God uses each of us differently, for different purposes. The key to take away concerning sermons is that they need to be focussed messages from God to the congregation through the pastor or other speaker.

At the end of a sermon, there may be an invitation or an altar call. This is an opportunity for the congregation to respond if the Holy Spirit has used the message to speak to their hearts. The pastor, or some of the church leaders, will stand at the front and will call for people to come to the altar. There, the pastor or the church leaders will pray with them.

They may need to be led to pray for salvation – giving up the wages of their sin for the gift of God, which is eternal life. They may need to renew their commitment to God. They may simply need prayer for a problem in their life. They may come forward to join the church, or to be baptized. While this is going on, the pastor will usually ask the praise team to play softly or to sing softly.

When all of the decisions have been made, and no one else is coming to the altar, the pastor will close the invitation. This will usually be a prayer. This is the end of the sermon portion.

The last part of the service is the benediction, which literally means, "the good speaking."

There may be some announcements. Hopefully these are brief and to the point. Whoever is leading the service will then call for a song, or possibly will pray. He may simply speak a blessing to the congregation, such as, "May the Lord bless you and keep you, and cause His face to shine upon you."

At this point, the service is over.

Um, wait. What about the thing with the crackers and the juice? Or didn't you mention baptisms?

Well, the service above was a description of a basic simple service. It's kind of the bare-bones outline. The Lord's Supper, or Communion, may be part of the service. Different churches observe this on different schedules. Some have communion weekly;

others monthly; some quarterly. A Lord's Supper service is sometimes slightly different from the basic service.

At a certain point in the service – it may be during the song service, or between the song service and the sermon, or it may be after the sermon – the speaker will call attention to a table that is at the front and that is usually covered with a white cloth. The deacons will come to the front, and will uncover the table. There will be small trays of tiny crackers, and there will be small plastic cups of grape juice.

It is important that the juice be red, and that it be grape juice. White grape juice, or apple juice, or persimmon-cranberry – no, those will not fit the symbolism.

The congregation is called into a time of contemplation, and asked to examine their consciences and to set right with God anything in their own lives that might interfere with their relationship with God. Then the juice and the crackers – one each – are distributed to the believers. As a rule, churches do not require that those who partake are members of that specific church. But it is a requirement that they have already chosen to take the gift that God gives, and to reject the wages of sin. Communion is reserved for Christians.

Often, the pastor will read or will quote from 1 Corinthians 11, in which Paul talks about the Lord's supper. At the pastor's direction the congregation eats the cracker in unison, as the pastor reads, "This is my body, broken for you. Do this in remembrance of me." The pastor then directs the congregation to drink the cup in unison, as the pastor reads, "This cup is the new covenant in My blood; do this, as often as you drink it, in remembrance of Me."

There will then be a prayer. Sometimes the pastor will copy the first communion service, in which the Bible says that they sang a hymn and departed. The congregation will be led in a song, and then will go their way. Other times, the service will simply resume.

This is not the only way to do this.

I have attended churches where the congregation was seated in a circle, and a round loaf of sourdough was passed from person to person, with each tearing off a piece. A "common cup" was also passed around, and the juice was sipped from one cup, as the disciples did at the last supper. I have been in services where the cup contained actual wine, instead of grape juice.

I have seen services in the more "liturgical" manner, in which the congregation lines up before the altar. Each is fed a cracker and given a sip from the chalice by a minister at the front of the church. As we discussed in the last chapter, it is important to distinguish the intrinsic parts from the arbitrary parts, in this as in the rest of the church. We must never place a tradition before heart-felt worship of the Living God.

The symbolism of this ritual is very complex.

Jesus led his disciples to do this on the night before He was crucified. He was trying to express to them that He was going to be crucified for their sins, and the sins of the world. He compared his body to the bread, and his blood to the wine they drank.

As a believer eats the bread and drinks the wine, he confesses his guilt. He is saying, in effect, that it was he who broke the body of Jesus and drew His blood. It was not nails that held Jesus to the cross: It was our sin. In taking part in this ritual, we are telling God that we killed his Son.

But we are also putting our faith in the crucifixion of Jesus to save us from our sins. We are covering our sin with the only cure for sin; His broken body and shed blood. We are confessing our sin and calling for its forgiveness in one gesture. And God is faithful and just, James tells us, to forgive us of our sin, and to cleanse us from all unrighteousness.

At the same time, we are taking in the body and blood of Christ and making it one with our bodies. We are acknowledging that Jesus is now a part of us, and lives through us. We are no longer who we once were. We've joined with Christ, and He is living through us.

More: We are acknowledging that we are now part of the body of Christ, the one single church that is composed of all believers, past, present, and future. We do not merely have a piece of Jesus' body and a bit of His blood; we are His body, and we are His blood. Jesus died, but He lives again, through us.

Finally, we are all parts of one body, and just as we are joined with the body of Jesus, we are all joined together with all other believers: one body, one church, with one common vision, and one common faith.

There is another ritual that we do, and that is baptism. Just as there are many ways to do the Lord's supper, there are many ways to do baptism. I personally believe that it should be done by dunking a person into water. We call that baptism by immersion.

Again, don't let traditions get in the way of Worship. I was taught, long ago, that baptism must be done with the right method (immersion, not sprinkling), the right medium (water, not oil), and the right meaning (a symbol, and not to save). But if a believer has been baptized by another method, with another medium – maybe the sign of the cross, marked on his forehead in oil – I will still call him my brother, so long as he believes on the Lord Jesus Christ.

Baptist by immersion is usually done in this manner:

The minister or other person conducting the baptism will stand in the pool, stream, river, or baptistry, if it is large enough, or else behind the tank or baptistry, if it is not. He will face the congregation. The person being baptized will enter the pool and stand in profile to the minister. In some cases, a seat is provided, under the water.

The minister may ask the person's name. This is a tradition based on the liturgical denominations, which assign a person's name on the day that he or she is baptized. Unless the person has a name that is compounded with a pagan god, or something of that nature, there is usually no need to assign a new name. But if the new believer is of a different culture, he or she may ask for a new "Christian" name.

The minister will then ask, "In Whom do you place your faith and trust?"

The expected answer is, "In Jesus Christ."

The minister will then say, "Upon your profession of faith, I baptize you now my brother [sister] in the name of the Father, and of the Son, and of the Holy Spirit." While saying this, the minister will use one hand to assist the person in laying back into the water until the head is covered. He will then help them to rise to a standing (or sitting) position.

While raising the person upright, the minister will say, "Buried with Christ in baptism, rise to walk in the newness of life."

We Baptists believe that a person should be baptized when he or she has made that commitment to reject the wages of sin and to accept God's gift of Eternal Life. Baptism is a symbol of that change.

In 2 Corinthians 5:17, Paul tells us that if anyone has believed in Jesus, he has become a new creature. The old creature is dead, and a new creature is born. Baptism is a symbol of that death and rebirth.

When we are baptized, we are symbolically saying that we have died. The person we used to be is dead. The water represents the grave; the end of that old life. Rising out of the water represents a new life as a Child of God, born anew. That is why the pastor will usually say, "Buried with Christ in beautiful baptism, rise to walk in the newness of life." But it is not just a symbol of our own life.

We are also recalling that Jesus died on the cross, was buried, rose on the third day, and was seen by many. We are acting out four of the five essential points of the gospel.

We are comparing what has happened to us – our new life in Christ – with what Jesus did for us. We are essentially saying that the same Person who rose from the dead will call us back out of our own graves. We are also acting out something that will happen on the last day, when we, like Christ, rise from our graves.

It is a simple act, but it has a very deep meaning.

Those two things, Baptism and the Lord's Supper, are the two ordinances of the church (that is, the things we are ordered to do as a church of believers).

We should also talk about three other kinds of meetings commonly held by churches: Prayer Meetings, Bible Studies, and Business Meetings. Once again, these are traditions, and you don't have to do it like this. This is how my church does things, but that's just tradition. If a different way works, then Glory to God; do it that way.

A Bible Study is a meeting for the purpose of studying the Bible. It can be incorporated into another form of meeting, such as a song service or a prayer meeting. It can also stand alone as the sole focus of the evening. A Bible study can be a book study, a topical study, or a historical study.

In a book study, the teacher would take a single book of the Bible and discuss its context within the Bible's historical framework, its authorship, and its purpose. The class might then (usually over the course of many meetings) analyze the book verse by verse, or chapter by chapter, bringing out the important points and applying those points to our daily lives and our interactions with God.

A Topical study will focus on a single subject, and will find references to that subject across the Bible. An example might be a study of references to Peace in the Bible. Or one might wish to find every reference to baptism, so that we can more fully understand how and why we baptize new believers.

As an example, there is a topical study of examples of salvation in appendix E, at the end of this book.

A historical study will focus on a period of Bible history, and will examine different accounts of that period found in different books of the Bible. One might also contrast the Bible account with secular history. For example, we might trace the missionary journeys of Paul, and compare his letters with the account in Acts, in order to determine what sites he visited and the years in which he did so.

A Bible study most often begins with prayer, and then the teacher will present the material that he or she has prepared for the study. At the end, a student will often be asked to close the meeting with another prayer.

Prayer meetings often have a Bible study element. For example, my church holds meetings on Tuesday Nights. They begin with a series of songs (two, sometimes three). The leader will then speak on a passage or on a topic, usually with a link to prayer. When he concludes, the prayer portion of the meeting will begin.

There may, optionally, be a time for the presentation of prayer requests. Some caution must be taken here: these must not turn into gossip sessions, and they must not be permitted to snowball until the time for actual prayer is taken up by discussion.

Prayer can be accomplished in any of several ways. The leader can pray aloud while the others pray silently. Or various people can pray aloud, one at a time, and when it seems as if everyone inclined to pray aloud has done so, the leader will pray, finishing with "Amen." Alternatively, everyone can pray aloud at the same time, or everyone can pray silently at the same time. Usually silent prayer is concluded by the leader praying aloud.

Another option is to break into smaller groups, each of which shares prayer concerns, and then prays "in a circle." In this style, one person will pray aloud, and when he or she says, "In Jesus' Name," the person to his left (or right, as arranged) will pray aloud, continuing around until everyone has prayed. The last person will say, "Amen."

Amen, incidentally, means something along the lines of "I completely agree" or "I join with my brother (or sister) in this prayer." Prayers are offered "In Jesus' Name" or "Through Jesus" as a recognition that we cannot enter the presence of God without Jesus acting as our High Priest and Advocate. Jesus commanded His disciples to pray in His Name.

We must be careful, of course, that when we pray in Jesus' Name, we pray only for things that Jesus would pray. We are telling God that we are asking for things that Jesus wants to see happen. That is a statement that we must not take lightly.

When the time of prayer is done, and the prayers have ended, the leader will conclude the service with a song, with a blessing, or with a short prayer.

Business meetings are held to conduct the business of the church. These are not religious in nature, though they will typically open and close with a brief prayer. They are usually held to address questions about the operation of the church, such as necessary repairs, election of leaders, and other practical things.

Business meetings are usually only held in churches that operate in a democratic fashion. Some churches are governed by a board of elders, who make all decisions. Other churches are governed by an organizational leader, such as a bishop.

In congregational-run churches, business meetings are necessary. They allow the church to make decisions about finances, leaders, schedules, and other matters. A set of strict rules will be followed, to make certain that everyone has an opportunity to speak, but that no one is allowed to dominate the meeting or to talk over others. Most churches adopt Robert's Rules of Order, Newly Revised. These rules determine who is to speak, how long they may speak, and who will speak next. They set guides for voting, for bringing new matters to the meeting, and for resolving old matters that have been discussed before.

In most cases, a business meeting will have a printed agenda. This is a list of things to be discussed. A typical agenda might look like this:

1. Call to Order
2. Reading of previous minutes
3. Acceptance or corrections to minutes
4. Reports from committees (teams) or officers
5. Old business
6. New business

7. Calendar
8. Closing of the Meeting (adjournment)

The Call to Order is merely the moderator (meeting leader) saying, "This meeting is now in session." It can be followed by a prayer. Usually, the leader calls on a specific person and asks that person to open in prayer.

The Clerk will then read the minutes of the previous meeting. The minutes are an outline of what was said and done at the previous meeting. Instead of reading the minutes, the clerk may hand out a written copy.

The people in the meeting are expected to make any corrections to the minutes that are necessary, such as "We scheduled the church picnic for Saturday, not Tuesday" or "Mr. Johnson's name is misspelled." When all necessary corrections are made, the minutes are declared to "Stand as read." This means that the minutes become an official record. It is not necessary to vote to accept the minutes, but many organizations do anyway.

After the minutes, reports will be given. The treasurer will usually give a financial statement, and explain any big changes in the church's financial condition. This will usually be accompanied by a printed financial report. Those present at the meeting will vote to accept the report.

Other leaders may give reports, as the moderator call on them. Committees (or teams) may also give reports. A report is merely a brief overview of what the team has done in the past month, what it expects to do in the next month, and any challenges that the team may face. Each report should be approved.

Old business will then be brought up. These items will each be listed on the agenda before the meeting. Anything that continues from one meeting to the next will be old business. For example, if the church is doing a construction project, updates to that project will be presented as old business.

New business items will also be listed in the agenda. These are items that have not been discussed before. An example might be a proposal that the church repave the parking lot, or that the men's ministry hold an event in a public park. These items should not be something just then introduced from the floor. The sponsors of these items should have given them to the church clerk in advance, and the church clerk should have placed these items on the agenda.

Before any item can be discussed, whether it is new or old business, it must first have a motion and a second. The motion is presented by saying, "I make a motion that we do this…" and the second consists of a second person saying, "I second the motion." Only after a motion and second can the item be discussed.

The goal of this rule – that any item requires a motion and a second before it can be discussed – is to prevent a single person from tying up the meeting by talking endlessly about something trivial. If an item of business comes from a committee, it is considered to already have a motion and second, because there are at least two people on the committee.

Next, there will usually be a brief discussion of items on the calendar. This is intended to avoid scheduling conflicts, and to make sure that events and meetings are held timely.

Finally, the moderator will close the meeting, either by declaring the meeting adjourned, or by asking someone present to "Close us in prayer."

It is the hope of all Christians that our meetings are orderly and reflect well upon the church and upon our God. Sadly, this is not always the case. Christians sometimes fail to live up to the standards we claim. There is no excuse for disorderly behavior in a meeting, regardless what kind of meeting it is.

But when it happens, keep in mind that Christians are not perfect. We are merely forgiven. We remain sinners, and while we strive to allow God to perfect us, we are still far from perfect.

At the risk of being redundant, the examples of methods above are just that: Examples. At one time, I used to attend church with a friend, who was of the Plymouth Brethren denomination. While I do not agree with all of their teachings, I did find their gatherings ("Assemblies," as they called them) to be refreshingly worshipful.

The congregation sat in a circle, or in concentric circles, as space allowed. Someone would stand and pray, then sit down again. This signaled the beginning of the service. From time to time, someone would stand up and ask us to sing a song from the hymnal with him, or to pray with him for a particular concern. Once in a while, someone would remark on something he had read in his daily devotions. At a certain point, someone would say, "Let us break the bread." A loaf of bread would be passed around, and each person would tear off a piece. In a similar way, the cup would be passed around.

Then someone would stand up and present a sermon. The sermon speaker was pre-arranged; The other parts – prayers, hymns, and remarks about the Word of God – were spontaneous, as each person felt led to share in the worship.

It was a particularly restful form of worship, and its lack of structure made it no less orderly. But again, that too was tradition, and not a divine decree. In the style of worship, there is not one right way to do things.

We must be careful that our worship doesn't mock God or take Him for granted. Worship must be focussed on God. We must guard against false teachers. But the exact style of worship that we use is not as important as the attitude of our hearts and the devotion of our minds.

Our methods may change over time, but our message must never change. The pre-Pauline doctrine is still the key teaching in the church, and must always be.

Another Elephant:

The sheer number of elephants involved in Christianity is staggering. Offerings are another such elephant.

Opinions with regard to tithes, tithing, and offerings in general run the gamut from "No one should give anything" to "Everyone should give everything." Well, neither of those is a practical option. If no one contributed anything, then the church would have trouble keeping the lights on. Candlelight services are nice, but even then, someone's got to buy the candles.

I knew one lady who felt that the pastor should live on nothing, and possibly take a bit of money from the offering each week so that he could eat a Sunday dinner. I don't think she really understood what a pastor really does for a church, nor that he would starve to death. I also once knew a man who, whenever tithing was mentioned, would get mad and walk home.

On the other hand, if everyone gave everything to the church, then they would neglect their Christian duties to feed themselves and their families. There are notable Christians who were known for their extreme generosity, of course, but this is not the expectation.

Nicholas of Myra was famous for Christian giving. He was born wealthy, but gave away his family fortune, bit by bit, giving gifts to feed the poor. When he had no more money of his own, he would borrow from his wealthy friends and give the money to the poor. When his friends caught on, and quit lending him money, he began disguising himself and begged in the streets, so that he could feed and clothe the poor.

Nicholas of Myra literally gave away all he had, and all that he could beg or borrow. For that reason he is still famous by another name, and is still associated with generosity. As a Christian example of love for his fellow man, and for living as a stranger on this planet – for we are not of this world – Saint Nick is still revered today.

Does God expect that of you? Not likely. It is more likely that God expects you to feed and clothe your family, and to shelter them, and to keep them warm. Still, all that you have is a gift from God, and it does acknowledge his providence when you give some of that to the work of the church, or to feed the poor around you.

How much? Well, that's a good question. The traditional answer is 10%, but that may be more than you can afford to give. Or God may have blessed you to the point that 10% means nothing to you. Paul made a remark in 2 Corinthians 9:7 that each person should do as he has purposed in his heart, neither grudgingly nor under compulsion, for the Lord loves a cheerful giver.

My view is this: When God blesses us, we should look for ministries where he is working, and we should join Him in that work by contributing a token of God's gift to us. In my case, that generally means 10% to the local church where I worship. Someone's got to keep the lights on.

I also give around 1% to a local ministry that works with the poor, and with addictions. I have carefully investigated them, know that they are solid and trustworthy, and I give a small portion of what I am blessed with because I like doing it. I like knowing that I have a small, even miniscule, part in the good work that they do. I feel good about giving it, which is what Paul means when he says to do as we have purposed in our heart, and that God loves a cheerful giver. No one makes me do it; I don't do it because I have to; and I won't feel bad if I can't, aside from wishing for that ministry to be richly blessed.

And as we said in an earlier chapter, good works are not something we do because they will save us, or even because they will please God. Works are a byproduct of being a Christian. When I get to heaven, and God asks why I deserve to come in, my answer will not be that I gave to the church, nor that I gave to the poor, nor that I gave to a particular ministry. It will be that Jesus died on the cross for my sins.

My works are nothing. Jesus is everything.

A Digression Concerning the Valley of Dry Bones

You may or may not be familiar with a passage in Ezekiel that is commonly referred to as the Valley of the Dry Bones. It is found in Ezekiel 37:1-14.

1 The hand of the LORD was upon me, and He brought me out by the Spirit of the LORD and set me down in the middle of the valley; and it was full of bones.

2 He caused me to pass among them round about, and behold, there were very many on the surface of the valley; and lo, they were very dry.

3 He said to me, "Son of man, can these bones live?" And I answered, "O Lord GOD, You know."

4 Again He said to me, "Prophesy over these bones and say to them, 'O dry bones, hear the word of the LORD.'

5 "Thus says the Lord GOD to these bones, 'Behold, I will cause breath to enter you that you may come to life.

6 'I will put sinews on you, make flesh grow back on you, cover you with skin and put breath in you that you may come alive; and you will know that I am the LORD.'"

7 So I prophesied as I was commanded; and as I prophesied, there was a noise, and behold, a rattling; and the bones came together, bone to its bone.

8 And I looked, and behold, sinews were on them, and flesh grew and skin covered them; but there was no breath in them.

9 Then He said to me, "Prophesy to the breath, prophesy, son of man, and say to the breath, 'Thus says the Lord GOD, "Come from the four winds, O breath, and breathe on these slain, that they come to life."'"

> *10 So I prophesied as He commanded me, and the breath came into them, and they came to life and stood on their feet, an exceedingly great army.*
>
> *11 Then He said to me, "Son of man, these bones are the whole house of Israel; behold, they say, 'Our bones are dried up and our hope has perished. We are completely cut off.'*
>
> *12 "Therefore prophesy and say to them, 'Thus says the Lord GOD, "Behold, I will open your graves and cause you to come up out of your graves, My people; and I will bring you into the land of Israel.*
>
> *13 "Then you will know that I am the LORD, when I have opened your graves and caused you to come up out of your graves, My people.*
>
> *14 "I will put My Spirit within you and you will come to life, and I will place you on your own land. Then you will know that I, the LORD, have spoken and done it," declares the LORD.'"*

Many sermons have been preached on the Valley of the Dry Bones, and many more will follow. It is an important passage of prophecy regarding the return of Israel from the Babylonian Captivity, and it is a prophecy about the work of Jesus Christ in the lives of believers, and it is a prophecy of the end times.

But I raise it here for none of those reasons.

There are two things I would like for us to understand about the church and about our walk within the church. First, there will be times when you go through a period of absolute deadness.

You won't be literally dead, but it will seem as if there is no life in what you are doing. Your circumstances will seem like a valley of dry bones. There will be no hope, nothing moving, nothing stirring, no sign of change. Do not despair.

Note the question that God asks of Ezekiel: "Son of man, can these bones live?"

Most of us would say, "No." The circumstances are hopeless. The job, the marriage, the career – it's dead. It's not just dead, but dead, and dried out, and all that is left is a pile of dry bones. But just a few nights ago, I heard a man talk about how his life was a broken mess, dried up and devoid of life, but that God used the book of Ezekiel to revive him.

I have heard many Christians talk about coming back from a circumstance that they thought was hopeless, and through God, seeing that circumstance utterly reversed. I know of examples in my own life where I believed that certain things were simply dead to me, or that certain relationships were hopelessly damaged. I have seen those things turn on a dime, by the hand of God.

I am not simply trying to bolster your courage; I am encouraging you to consider the Valley of the Dry Bones when you next feel that utter hopelessness. Notice the answer that Ezekiel gives: "Thou knowest, O Lord." We do not know the end. We cannot see how things will come about. But God does.

At this point, God commands Ezekiel to speak to the dry bones, and to promise them new life. The promise does not come from Ezekiel, but from God.

Next, the bones begin to move, and sinews begin to grow, then muscles, and then skin. Finally, God tells the prophet to call for the wind to breathe the breath of life into the bodies, and they begin to come alive.

Hopeless situations, under God's command, turn around in that way. We hear God's instruction, we follow God's instructions, and the pieces will begin to come together. New growth will follow, strength will return, and in a few minutes (seemingly), the entire landscape will be transformed.

Never despair. So long as you are a child of God, never despair. The Apostle Paul wrote this to those suffering persecution at Corinth (2 Cor. 4:7-10):

7 But we have this treasure in earthen vessels, that the excellency of the power may be of God, and not of us.

8 We are troubled on every side, yet not distressed; we are perplexed, but not in despair;

9 Persecuted, but not forsaken; cast down, but not destroyed;

10 Always bearing about in the body the dying of the Lord Jesus, that the life also of Jesus might be made manifest in our body.

If we have the treasure of the gospel in our jars-of-clay bodies, nothing can destroy us; not really. God is at work in our lives, restoring us, holding us together, keeping us strong.

The second point I would draw from the Valley of Dry Bones is that we may find ourselves in a dry and dead ministry. We may find ourselves in a church like the church at Sardis, in Revelation 3, which Jesus rebuked, "You have a Name that you are alive, but you are dead."

God willing, you will never be in such a church or such a ministry. May God richly bless the work you do in His Name. But there are such churches, and such ministries. Out of mercy and godly restraint, I will not tell you stories about them.

But should you find yourself in such a place, do not despair. When you look around and say, "This congregation has fallen asleep, and even the last trumpet may not wake them," even then, do not despair.

It may be that God is calling you to a different place of ministry, where you can use your spiritual gifts to glorify God. It may be a signal that it's time to move on. Pray, read the word, speak to godly friends, and watch your circumstances.

But it may also be that God intends to use you in a mighty way. I know a man, whom I shall not name. He was given a small class to teach, in a small church, where the median age was 50-something, and the entire congregation numbered fewer than 50. The baptistry had not been wet in several years. There were no new ministries, there was no impetus to start ministries, and there was great resistance to any new ideas.

But God gave this man a place of service among the dry bones. This man resolved that he would systematically build that class; that he would use his talents to serve God, rather than hiding them in a napkin.

He made sacrifices. He spent his time and his money to make the ministry grow. He prayed hard, and he worked hard. Above all else, he called the power of God into that ministry. And that class began to grow.

Three became six. Coincidence, happenstance, surely it would have happened anyway, right? But six became twelve. Twelve became twenty-four. And suddenly this one small group dominated this tiny church.

The man began to call other leaders from the congregation alongside him, to help him. God blessed their works as well, and they were able to use their own talents in the service of God. Souls began to be saved.

In time, the church called a new minister, who began to powerfully share the word of God, and to systematically work to bring new growth in the church. Soon all of the ministries of the church were feeling new life, and the entire church began to grow. A church that once struggled to see 40 people for a Sunday service began to see hundreds.

And souls began to be saved. In one year, there were 25 baptisms; the following year there were 50. This, in a church that had once been barely alive – Not only did they have a Name that they were alive, but they were truly alive.

So what moved the dry bones? How did they come alive? First, the word of God was spoken to them. Then, they moved into a right relationship with each other. In the words of the old song, the toe-bone connected to the foot-bone. In a church – remember that we've spoken of a church being like a body, with many body parts – this would be manifest in people forgiving each other of old grudges. It would be seen in people laying down their fights over silly and pointless things.

As the bones came into the right relationships with each other, growth began to happen. The bones began to be connected by powerful sinews. In our metaphor, this would be a connection between members, born out of the common goal of praying and working together in ministry. Muscles grew; the bones became strong and powerful.

Where did the strength come from? It was a miracle of God brought about through the unity of the pieces of the body. As they became one, God gave them strength.

The finishing touches will come in due time: The skin, the hair, the fingernails. But then comes the greatest miracle: When God breathes new life into a ministry. It is a wonderful thing to see, when Jesus takes something broken and hopeless, and restores it to new service.

It is not always so. There are times when the bones refuse to come together. There are times when no effort and no prayer can move the hard hearts of Christians. It breaks the heart to think of it; that some Christians will not even listen to the word of the Lord.

But I must be honest and tell you that the Church at Sardis is still among us. I know a man, whom I shall not name. He found himself in the church of the Valley of the Dry Bones. He prayed that God would bring new growth. He prayed desperately that God would restore the church.

He worked. He took on ministries, he encouraged others in ministries, and bore every burden that he could on behalf of the church. He cried out to God for that church. In the end, it was not enough, and the church closed its doors.

The message from God for that man at that time was not to prophesy to the dry bones. Instead, God's message to him was "Why do you seek the Living among the dead?" (Luke 24:5). There comes a time when a ministry has served its purpose, and is no longer a useful tool for God to use. And when that happens, all that we can do is to leave it behind us.

But God is faithful. Leaving behind that ministry, leaving those dry bones to bury their own dead, he came to another church where God was working, and through that church God restored his hope, and gave him an effective place of ministry.

I say all of that to say this: When you find yourself in a personal dry place, do not despair. God is faithful. When you find yourself in a dry place of ministry, do not despair. Your tears are never in vain, and you are never alone. God is always faithful.

STAGE SIX
Going Deeper into the Faith:

WE SPOKE EARLIER about how Christian maturity comes naturally and organically from reading our Bibles and praying. But how do we learn to pray, and how do we learn more about our Bibles? Well, the answers are praying with other people, and reading the Bible with other people.

Find a Bible study that is based on reading the Word of God and learning to live by what it says. Be careful; there are many false teachers out there. But a good Bible study is worth its weight in gold, and learning the Word of God is like a treasure in your heart.

How will you know that the teacher is trustworthy?

1. Look for the fruit of the Spirit in his life. Earlier, we talked about these: Galatians 5:22-23 tells us that the fruit of the Spirit are love, joy, peace, patience, kindness, goodness, faithfulness, gentleness, and self-control; against these there is no law. Do you see these in the Bible study teacher?

2. By now, you will have spent a lot of time reading the Bible and praying. How well does your Bible reading and prayer match what the teacher is saying? In Acts, Paul praises a group of people known as the Bereans, because after he would preach, they would read the scriptures to see if his teaching matched what the scriptures said.

3. Check with Godly friends. Friends who, like you, are practicing the Word of God in their lives will also have the indwelling Spirit of God speaking to them and through them. Do they agree with these teachings?

4. Look for the warning signs of false teachers. Many books of the New Testament warn against false teachers, who build themselves up. Read these passages and look for danger signs. Does the teacher tell you to seek material wealth? Paul tells us in Colossians to set our eyes on things eternal. Does the teacher tell you that Jesus will return on a certain day? Jesus tells us in Matthew that no man knows the day, nor the hour.

If a leader tells you that you need to place your faith in him, or that his teachings or his role in the kingdom of God is unique in some way, run from him. If a teacher claims that only those who believe his teachings will be saved, run from him. If a leader holds a different standard for himself than he does for others, or claims that he has a special dispensation to do things that are not permitted for other people, run from him.

If a leader introduces another writer and sets that writer's teachings on the same level as those of Jesus, you need to leave at once. The 66 books that are in the Bible – and some denominations also use a handful of other writings called the apochrypha – are all the books that you need. If a teacher tells you that there are books missing from the Bible, this is a sign of a false teacher.

There are some books mentioned in the Bible that are not a part of the Bible. For example, in some of the historical books, you will hear mention of parallel accounts in the records of other nations' kings. This is a bit like me saying that you might have read of a certain occurrence in the newspaper. I am not thereby telling you that the newspapers are a part of *this* book, nor that the newspapers are reliable guides about *this* book.

Do not allow the mention of a "Book of Enoch," for example (because James cites a quote from Enoch in James' New Testament letter to the churches) to make you wonder if the Bible has been altered. The short answer is, no, what you see is what's there. Beware of false teachers who would use this to divert you from Bible study into the study of some other teaching.

That's not to say that such a teaching might not be enlightening. There may be some insight into the historical and spiritual background of the times. A certain man recently used a reference in the Book of Enoch as food for thought regarding a subject we were discussing, and the passage was noteworthy. Still, books that cannot be firmly placed in the canon need to be held apart from books that can.

I do not accept the Apochrypha as scripture (other Christians do) and yet I believe that there are some good Christian lessons to be learned in the Apochrypha. We can learn about God, and allow him to speak to us, through even dubious writings. But in my opinion, the Apochrypha are not the word of God.

There are some excellent books that illuminate Christian Bible study, such as Matthew Henry's commentary. Matthew Henry was an eighteenth-century preacher who had studied the Word of God extensively, and who was given wisdom by God to reveal the truth of scripture. He wrote six volumes about the Bible, taking each verse and pointing out the key things we should observe in that passage. One of my favorite quotes is something he wrote about Genesis 1:1, where we learn that in the beginning, God created the heavens and the earth. Henry says,

> *Let us learn hence: That atheism is folly, and the atheist the greatest fool in nature, for he lives in a world that could not make itself, and yet he will not own it had a maker.*

There is great wisdom to be found in Henry's writings. I have also found other Christian writers to be good spiritual guides, such as C. S. Lewis (one of the most famous of modern Christian writers). His books, *Mere Christianity* and *The Screwtape Letters* deserve special mention.

G. K. Chesterton's *The Everlasting Man* and his *Orthodoxy* deserve to be mentioned. Dorothy L. Sayers' *The Whimsical Christian* is a fun read. Max Lucado's *Cure for the Common Life* is a good start. None of these can replace the Bible itself, and all of these are valuable to Christians only insofar as they reflect upon the Bible.

These are not dangerous books. Reading or even studying them can be enlightening. But they are not the Bible.

The danger comes when a book not only illuminates scripture and Godly living, but is placed on the same level and given the same authority as scripture. If I place the writings of Alphaeus Cutler, for example, or the *Encyclopedia Britannica*, or Edward Gibbon's *Decline and Fall of the Roman Empire* – or any other writing whatsoever – on a par with the Bible, then I have stopped practicing Christianity. At that point, I will have become a heretic.

Learning to discern sound teachers (who teach the Bible without adding in other books of so-called scripture) from false teachers (who distract from the Bible and divert people from the Bible) will go far in expanding your faith. There is another danger, of course, and that is to become so exact in your doctrine that you stop loving God and your fellow Christians. This was the error of the Church at Ephesus.

Hopefully, your church conducts Bible studies and regular discussions about the Bible, giving you the opportunity to learn more, in depth. Your church leaders can also help you to find Bible studies that will build up your faith.

The key is this: You need to not merely read the Bible, but to actually study it. In the past, Christians used to memorize passages from the Bible, on the grounds that they might not have their Bibles with them when they need that one particular passage that they needed. When Jesus was tempted by the devil, He rebuked him by quoting scripture.

Memorized scripture is a powerful tool in the hands of a Christian. Hebrews 4:12 tells us that the word of God is *alive and active; Sharper than any double-edged sword, penetrating even to dividing soul and spirit, joints and marrow; it judges the thoughts and attitudes of the heart.* So we might reasonably think of memorized scripture as a hidden weapon in our spiritual battles.

When the enemy seems to have us surrounded, we are never disarmed. When the world is dark, we are never without a light. When we don't see the right way to proceed, there is a source of powerful wisdom at our fingertips.

Memorize Matthew 6:33, and use it when you are tempted by worldly wealth. Memorize Romans 6:23. Spend some time thinking about the contrast between a wage and a gift. Memorize Galatians 5:22-23. Ask yourself if those are the fruit that are growing in your life. Memorize Isaiah 53:5-6. Ask yourself if you, like a sheep, have gone astray, seeking your own way, though the LORD has laid the iniquity of us all onto Jesus.

I have a favorite story about scripture memory. Once long ago, I taught Sunday School (a form of Bible study) for teenagers. There was a young man who only attended because he liked a certain girl there. We'll call them Mike and Jenny. Jenny's parents did not allow her to date, but she was allowed to go to church events.

There was an event called Scripture Memory Pizza. Once a quarter, kids who recited a certain set of scriptures would be taken for pizza after church. Mike and Jenny each memorized all the scriptures to be able to go. This allowed them to see each other without actually being on a date, since it was a church event.

As they met with me to recite the last passage that they needed – Isaiah 53:4-6 – Jenny said, "I don't get that passage." Mike agreed that he didn't understand it either. I explained that Isaiah, 500 years before Jesus, had prophesied that God would place our sins onto Jesus, and that "by His stripes, we [would be] healed." Mike gave me an odd look, and then we all went to the church service.

The speaker that week said that he had felt especially impressed to preach on a certain passage that week, and began to talk about Romans 6:23, another verse they had learned. He talked about Isaiah 53:6, repeating what I had told them about Jesus' sacrifice. I hadn't tipped him off about Mike and Jenny, but he taught from nearly every scripture on the pizza list.

As the speaker was shaking hands with the congregation after the service, he stopped Mike and said, "Mike, you seem troubled." There, in the doorway of the church, he explained to Mike how to make Jesus his savior, and to become a child of God.

Memorizing scripture moved Mike from death into life.

It is not just a nice saying, that the Word of God is alive and active. It is a literal truth. Exposure to God's Word will change your life. That is why prayer and regular Bible reading are the key elements of Christian growth.

There is a group of Christians called the Gideons who devote themselves to spreading the Word of God by placing Bibles into hotel rooms. Their logic is that many people find themselves alone and desperate in a hotel room, and to find a Bible at such a moment may save their lives and their souls.

Gideons also give Bibles to service personnel and they sponsor events that hinge upon the Word of God. Why do they put such emphasis on the Bible? Because it is alive and active, and sharper than any two-edged sword.

We do not merely have a sword; we also have armor. In Galatians 6:13-17, Paul tells us to put on the armor of God. He describes it like this:

* The belt of truth
* The breastplate of righteousness
* The sandals of the preparation of the gospel
* The shield of faith
* The helmet of salvation
* The sword of the Spirit, which is the Word of God.

The belt of truth, to the Ephesians, would have been a thick leather skirt that protected the loins and the upper legs. Putting this in practical terms, this means that we need to try to be open and honest in our dealings with others. This will keep us from being attacked where we are the most vulnerable. Remember back in Stage 1, where we talked about acting justly?

The breastplate of righteousness: This we should envision as a bronze plate that covers our chest and our stomach. This plate represents righteousness. We talked earlier about how we cannot be righteous in our own power. Instead we are righteous if, and only if, Jesus has placed His righteousness upon us. In other words, acting justly through the power of Jesus, and not by our own efforts.

The sandals of the preparation of the gospel of peace would be a thick leather slab strapped firmly to the feet. We are able to move forward with presenting the gospel only if we are prepared. That is, if we have been reading the Bible and learning from it, so that we are ready to give an answer for what we believe and why we believe it. This kind of preparation will protect us from thorns and rocks – from the obstacles that we may find in our paths as we share the good news of Jesus.

The shield of faith – knowing what we believe and why we believe it, and being confident in that knowledge – will save us from the "fiery darts" of the evil one. The accuser will throw doubts at us. He will attempt to pierce us with memories of things we did or did not say or do. He will try to make us question God's love for us. We may even be tempted to doubt whether God has the power to save us.

The shield of faith will keep these from penetrating to our vulnerable places. We spoke earlier about the nature of faith – what it means, and how to know that our faith is reasonable. Again, knowing what you believe and why you believe it, which comes from reading and studying the Bible, will protect you from lies of the enemy.

The helmet of salvation – I often wonder why Paul didn't mention this first, since it is the most basic item. Salvation comes from faith in Jesus Christ. The helmet protects your head. It is the single most important piece of armor. In our case, that is our salvation. Having saving faith in Jesus Christ moves us from death to life. Without that kind of faith, the rest is pointless.

And finally, we come to the sword of the Spirit, which is the Word of God. In other words, reading your Bible. Studying your Bible. Memorizing it; hiding it in your heart. As a soldier trains with his rifle or his sword until it is an extension of his arm, so we need to train with our Bibles until they are an extension of our hearts.

In case you're hard of reading, and have missed the point until now, read your Bible and pray.

Study the Word. Go deep into it. Meet God there.

Some Stage Six Teachings

Over the centuries, as people have studied the Word of God and tried to apply it to their lives, questions have arisen about exactly what they should believe on various topics. To answer these questions, wise men have composed statements of faith, sometimes called creeds.

One such creed is called the Apostles' Creed. It goes like this:

1. I believe in God the Father, Almighty, Maker of heaven and earth:
2. And in Jesus Christ, his only begotten Son, our Lord:
3. Who was conceived by the Holy Ghost, born of the Virgin Mary:
4. Suffered under Pontius Pilate; was crucified, dead and buried: He descended into hell:
5. The third day he rose again from the dead:
6. He ascended into heaven, and sits at the right hand of God the Father Almighty:
7. From thence he shall come to judge the quick and the dead:
8. I believe in the Holy Ghost:
9. I believe in the holy catholic church: the communion of saints:
10. The forgiveness of sins:
11. The resurrection of the body:
12. And the life everlasting. Amen.

I must quickly clarify that the word "catholic" used in the ninth item does not refer to the catholic denominations. It instead means "All-encompassing."

The creed above explains many basic Christian teachings in a few easy-to-remember phrases. It doesn't explain how to be saved. It's useful, but it's not everything that Christians teach.

A more detailed statement can be found in the Nicene Creed:

I believe in one God, the Father Almighty, Maker of heaven and earth, and of all things visible and invisible.

And in one Lord Jesus Christ, the only-begotten Son of God, begotten of the Father before all worlds; God of God, Light of Light, very God of very God; begotten, not made, being of one substance with the Father, by whom all things were made.

Who, for us men for our salvation, came down from heaven, and was incarnate by the Holy Spirit of the virgin Mary, and was made man; and was crucified also for us under Pontius Pilate; He suffered and was buried; and the third day He rose again, according to the Scriptures; and ascended into heaven, and sits on the right hand of the Father; and He shall come again, with glory, to judge the quick and the dead; whose kingdom shall have no end.

And I believe in the Holy Ghost, the Lord and Giver of Life; who proceeds from the Father and the Son; who with the Father and the Son together is worshipped and glorified; who spoke by the prophets.

And I believe one holy catholic and apostolic Church. I acknowledge one baptism for the remission of sins; and I look for the resurrection of the dead, and the life of the world to come. Amen.

This is a very strong teaching. Remember stage 0, where we talked about the pre-Pauline gospel? It had five points: That Jesus died for the sins of mankind, was buried, rose from the dead, was seen by many, and shall return on the last day.

Four of these five points are spelled out in this creed, in the third paragraph: *Who, for us men for our salvation, ... was made man; and was crucified also ... and was buried; and the third day He rose again, ... and He shall come again, with glory, to judge the quick and the dead; whose kingdom shall have no end.*

The Nicene Creed does not expressly state that Jesus was seen by many. But it has the pre-Pauline creed embedded in it. Those same points are also in the Apostles' Creed, except that it doesn't say that Jesus died for the sins of Mankind.

Keep in mind that these Creeds are not a replacement for the scripture. Knowing that the Nicene Creed says that Jesus was very God of very God does not replace reading in John 1:1-5, that

1. In the beginning was the Word, and the Word was with God, and the Word was God.
2. The Same was in the beginning with God.
3. By Him were all things made, and without Him was not anything made which was made.
4. In him was life, and the life was the light of men,
5. And the light shines in the darkness, and the darkness overcomes it not.

The creeds derive from, but do not replace, passages such as Colossians 1:17,

17. And He is before all things, and in Him all things consist.

We have to be careful that we do not set anything on an equal basis with the Word of God. No teaching, however inspirational, is the inspired Word of God, except the Bible itself. We must never place traditions of men above the Bible. Nonetheless, the creeds can be a powerful tool for understanding and summarizing what we believe about God.

STAGE SEVEN
Failing in the Faith

OKAY, HONESTLY, FAILURE is not supposed to be a stage in our Christian lives. But it happens. We are human beings, and we have not yet been perfected by God. Does that mean that we are failures, and that God will cast us out?

No. It means that we failed, and we need to ask God to forgive us. That's all. We start again.

We talked about this in Stage 3. So why do we need to go deeper on the topic now? Well, because we keep on sinning. It's not a one and done – oh, if that were only the case – but it's more like a forest fire: When we sin, we start it burning all over again.

So let's talk about fire fighting – using the shield of faith to extinguish the fiery darts of the evil one (Ephesians 6:16).

God loved us when we were sinners in the first place. He will not stop loving us because we failed yet again. Paul writes that he is convinced that nothing can separate us from the love of God through Jesus Christ:

> Romans 8:37-39
> *37 Nay, in all these things we are more than conquerors through him that loved us.*
> *38 For I am persuaded, that neither death, nor life, nor angels, nor principalities, nor powers, nor things present, nor things to come,*

39 Nor height, nor depth, nor any other creature, shall be able to separate us from the love of God, which is in Christ Jesus our Lord.

Okay, let's count things that can not separate us from the love of God: Death, Life, Angels, Kingdoms, Powers, the Present, the Past, height, depth, any creature... So that pretty much covers everything. By the way, I would encourage you to read the sixth, seventh, and eighth chapters of Romans all in one go. It's a great lesson on sin, and on how we ought to deal with it.

As you read those three chapters, notice what Paul says about continuing to sin. We are no longer under the law – in other words, we're free from the penalty of sin. So should we keep sinning, just because we're not bound by the law?

Of course not, says Paul. We are not slaves of sin any more, so we should not live like slaves of sin. Instead, we are now slaves of righteousness. We're addicted to Grace (Romans 6:15-23).

Paul asks another question, and it might seem a bit strange to us today. He says, "So should we keep sinning so that grace may abound?" And of course, the answer is "No."

There were people in Paul's time who reasoned like this: Jesus' gift to us – His grace – is huge because the sum of all our sins was huge. So that means that if we sin more, then the gift Jesus gave us is bigger. So we're helping God, right? Um, no. Just, no.

Paul tells us that when we were baptized, we demonstrated our own death, and the death of Jesus – we took part in His death, burial and resurrection. But someone who dies – as we symbolically died – is freed from sin. We can't commit sins of the flesh if our flesh is dead. We can't be controlled by carnal thoughts if our brains are dead to sin (see Romans 6:1-3,7).

So are we supposed to sin – to hurt people, to hurt ourselves, to chase after earthly pleasures? No, obviously not. We're supposed to be dead to that. That doesn't mean that we are never tempted to sin – we're sin addicts, and sin is always tempting us. What it means is that just as we were freed from the penalty of sin, we are now being progressively freed from the power of sin. And one day, when we die or when Christ comes again, we will be freed from the presence of sin.

So are we supposed to try really, really, hard not to sin? Well, we're supposed to try. We're not supposed to set ourselves up to fail. If, in the past, your major sin was drunkenness, then you need to plan a route home from work that doesn't take you past bars and liquor stores. But sometimes you will fail. When you do, the most important thing is that you talk it over with God, ask forgiveness, and keep trying.

We sometimes talk about the church as a hospital for sinners. Even those of us who are being treated for sin, and who have been undergoing treatment for a long time – we are still sinners. The church is not a hall of saints, where people go when they've gotten too good to sin. If it were, we wouldn't have anyone in the church.

Instead, the church is a sin clinic and those of us who have been here the longest are helping to change the bandages of those who have come in more recently. We cannot heal sin – only Jesus can do that. We can only bring people to Him, so that He can heal them of sin.

Or, to see it another way: the church is like a twelve-step program for sin. We bring sinners and guide them to acknowledge that they are sinners, and that they cannot control their sin. We teach them that only the High Power of Jesus Christ can give them the strength to overcome, and we encourage them to call on Him. We try to make right the things that we've done wrong. We try to guide others to overcome sin.

Daily we live, day by day, always trying to be more like Jesus. One day, we will be like him. One day, we will see him face to face. For now, we can only be His hospital, or his twelve-step method.

So how, in practical terms, do we overcome sin?

Well, as with a twelve-step program, one day at a time. We work on not sinning this time – not saying a bad word when this driver cuts us off in traffic this time; not being angry when that coworker drops the ball this time – and a continuous chain of "Not this time" turns into "not today" and then "not this week."

A Christian brother who is an alcoholic spoke with me this week and talked about his first time at a meeting where tokens were being given to those who had been sober for certain times. He despaired that while some were sober one month, two months, a year, or longer, he himself was only sober a few days.

But then one day he found himself at another meeting, and realized that he had been sober for ten years. The path from sin is that same kind of progress: A day at a time, with no real markers and no real signposts. Then, one day, we suddenly find, to our own surprise, that we have come a long way from where we once were.

It is helpful to understand how sin develops, as this makes it easier to nip it in the bud, or to recognize it when it starts. Consider James 1:14-15:

> *14But each one is tempted when by his own evil desires he is lured away and enticed.*
> *15Then after desire has conceived, it gives birth to sin; and when sin is fully grown, it gives birth to death.*

James gives us a picture of sin developing as a series of steps: First we are lured away and enticed by our own evil desires (v.14). Think of this as seeing something that we desire – money, for example. We stop thinking of what God wants and we start thinking of what we want. James compares this to sin being "conceived."

Next, James tells us, desire gives birth to sin. We see money, we are enticed by it, we conceive a plan for getting it, and we decide to steal it. Desire has given birth to sin – we are now making plans for how we might fulfill that desire. And then that sin, when it is fully grown, gives birth to death. We actually complete our plan, and steal. This brings the death of the relationship with the victim of our theft, it brings the death of safety in our community, and it brings death to a part of our own souls.

Desire, then concept, then plan, then fulfillment, then death. Five stages of sinning.

So what do we do? Well, what if we looked at worldly wealth, and for all of its power, considered instead that it will never give us the things we really need? This would stop the desire for money from driving us onward.

What if we refused to make a plan to steal? When the concept comes to us, what if we reject it and refuse to think about it? A wise man once said that we cannot prevent birds from flying over our heads, but we can prevent them from making nests in our hair. In the same way, the idea to sin – in this example, to steal something – may pop into our minds. But we can refuse to give it a home there.

Again, it is important to understand that sin works in secret. When we turn the light onto it, and look directly at it, we rob sin of its power over us. When we realize that we have an unhealthy desire – for money, for power, for the flesh – we have an opportunity to stop the process before it starts.

When we find that we have unhealthy concepts popping into our minds, we can ask the Holy Spirit to show us the unhealthy desires from which these concepts are originating. Keep in mind that sinful desires have good things at their root; the problem is not the desire but rather having the desire in an unhealthy way. Food is not sin; obsession with food to the point of gluttony is sin. Money is not evil; an unhealthy desire for money – to the point that we would plan to lie, cheat, and steal for it – is evil.

When we find that we are actually making plans to sin – imagining how we might, if we were less honest, of course – how we might easily steal that one thing that we really desire – not that we'd ever do it, you understand… See how we lie to ourselves, in order to allow the plan to grow? That's what happens when we have allowed the concept into our minds. When we find this kind of reasoning going on in our heads, we need to stop and examine it. We need to ask why we're planning sin, if we're never going to do it. The light of introspection and prayer is vitally important.

Again, remember what we have said before – God convicts us to correct us. The Holy Spirit shows us the unhealthy desire so that we can surrender that desire to God. We confront it, ask God to heal it, and keep an eye on it to make sure it doesn't sneak back into our lives. Thus, we slowly, carefully, with many wrong turns and false starts, learn over the course of our lives, one day at a time, to defeat the power of sin.

The accuser, by contrast, condemns us to destroy us. When we turn our attention to the unhealthy desires we wish to overcome, the accuser will say things like, "What an evil person you are, to want such things! How can you call yourself a Christian and think about things like THAT!"

The accuser wishes for us to hide the shame of our sin in dark places in our hearts, so that it will fester and continue to grow. Instead of confronting it and warily guarding against it in the future, the accuser wishes us to keep our eyes on the past and to ignore the painful secret sin that is taking over our present lives. We need the antiseptic of daylight – looking at our desires and our sins openly before God, so that He can heal them. We must confess our sins to God, and open our hearts to His healing.

Let's look at what happened to one sinner who stood accused before God:

> Zechariah 3:1-5 (NASB)
> *1 Then he showed me Joshua the high priest standing before the angel of the LORD, and Satan standing at his right hand to accuse him.*
> *2 The LORD said to Satan, "The LORD rebuke you, Satan! Indeed, the LORD who has chosen Jerusalem rebuke you! Is this not a brand plucked from the fire?"*
> *3 Now Joshua was clothed with filthy garments and standing before the angel.*
> *4 He spoke and said to those who were standing before him, saying, "Remove the filthy garments from him." Again he said to him, "See, I have taken your iniquity away from you and will clothe you with festal robes."*
> *5 Then I said, "Let them put a clean turban on his head." So they put a clean turban on his head and clothed him with garments, while the angel of the LORD was standing by.*

What is remarkable here to me is that Joshua was guilty. His clothes were dirty, a metaphor used throughout the Bible for sin. But God ordered the removal of his sin, and the accuser was rebuked. Joshua, undeserving though he was, had his sins forgiven.

God's grace is the cure, not any effort or trying harder on our part. We must never give up, but it's not done by our effort, but by God's grace. Works will not save us. Only God can do that.

Another remarkable thing is that the accuser, no doubt, wanted Joshua to hide from God, and to try to cover up his dirty clothes. The accuser wanted him to be afraid of facing God. But instead, Joshua stood before God and was made clean. God did not say a harsh word to Joshua about his sins, but instead assured

Joshua that through his leadership, God's blessings would come to the people – and even, in time, the Messiah.

What do we do when we become aware of evil in our thoughts? Turn it over to God. Stand before Him: Pray about it. Read the Bible. Refuse to indulge the process of sin. And when we fail – start over. Trust in the grace of God through Jesus.

We do not need to be afraid of God, even when we have sinned. Compare Romans 8:15. Continue to go to God with your failures, and let Him make them right.

As we go through this process of sinning, failing, and repenting, we begin to learn that the objects of our desires are tepid and tasteless. We begin to learn that our concepts of fulfilling our sinful wishes are silly and weak. We begin to learn that allowing those concepts to grow into plans will not fulfill us, or give us what we truly want and need – those things are found only in Jesus.

We begin to learn, from cycles of sin, that true fulfillment comes only through God. Only through our relationship with Jesus will we find the true desires of our heart – the good, true, faithful, correct and proper desires of a pure heart, devoted to God.

If only we could learn that to start with…

STAGE EIGHT
All the Rest of the faith.

AND NOW, IT'S TIME to face the herd of pachyderms that have been haunting our steps for the entire book. After all, there's a lot more to Christianity than what we've talked about here. Well, sort of.

On the one hand, the central truths of Christianity are exactly as simple as Stage Zero made them. But on the other hand, that's not all, and if we left it there without discussing some of the other things, we'd be trampled by all the elephants in the room. The most important things are the ones we've already discussed, and those lay a foundation for the remainder.

But now, in the words of the Apostle Paul, *"Allow me to show you a more excellent way."* (1 Cor. 12:31).

In First Corinthians, and again in other passages, Paul speaks of something known as spiritual gifts. You will find that churches look at spiritual gifts as something of a hot potato; in many ways, we really don't know how to deal with them.

1 Cor. 12:1 begins with Paul describing what spiritual gifts are, and how they work to edify (build up) the church. In short, when Jesus said His farewell to His disciples and rose into the sky, He promised that He would send the Holy Spirit to dwell within them. It's a strange concept, to have the Spirit of God living within a human body. But that's what Jesus promised, and that's what happened. And that is why, as a Christian, you typically feel two kinds of impulses at any given time: An impulse to do good and Godly things, to seek God, to love people – and at the same time,

an impulse to please your own flesh, to see out things of this world, and to desire power.

You have your human nature, and the Holy Spirit of God, both at the same time, living in your body. Maybe that explains some things about why you often feel conflicted about sin. Paul even wrote in Romans 7 about how he found himself doing things he knew he shouldn't, and not doing the things he knew he should. So if Paul understood that conflict, maybe we should also understand it.

But the gift of the Holy Spirit is not just a single thing: The Holy Spirit Himself also gives us gifts, or supernatural abilities, to lift up the church and to Glorify God. That part is pretty well understood in the Bible, and agreed upon throughout the church.

The potential for conflict comes in when we try to understand those gifts. Some of the gifts Paul mentions in First Corinthians are pretty obvious and easy to understand. Some people have the gift of preaching, or exhortation. Some people have the gift of teaching, or taking complex things and making them clear to everyone. Some people have gifts in the ability to comfort people, to be patient with people, to be kind to people. Some people are gifted leaders and gifted administrators. Those gifts are easy to understand.

But there are also gifts such as speaking in tongues. We see this gift in Acts, when the followers of Jesus began to speak in languages that they did not know, and the people visiting Jerusalem from all around the world each were able to hear about Christ in their own language. Paul also speaks of tongues as a prayer language, and in 1 Cor. 13:1, he uses the phrase, "*Though I speak with the tongues of men and of angels,*" implying that there is a language used in heaven that is different from earthly speech.

There are gifts such as healing, and gifts such as prophecy, the word of knowledge, and the word of wisdom – frankly, it's not always clear how each of these is used by the Spirit to edify the church, but when used correctly and appropriately, they do.

Yes, I used that phrase, "correctly and appropriately." That implies that these may be used inappropriately and incorrectly. And that also is true.

I attended a church service once in which many people prayed all at once, all of them speaking in syllables that did not resemble any language with which I am familiar. No one made an effort to translate, and no one made an effort to moderate. To my ear, it sounded like gibberish.

I cannot see inside another person's heart, and I do not know if these brethren were sincere, or were seeking God's heart, or were merely playing along with a charade. It's not for me to say. What I can say is that the display was not in accordance with the Bible.

> [1Co 14:27-29 NASB]
> *27 If anyone speaks in a tongue, it should be by two or at the most three, and each in turn, and one must interpret;*
> *28 but if there is no interpreter, he must keep silent in the church; and let him speak to himself and to God.*
> *29 Let two or three prophets speak, and let the others pass judgment.*

Two or three people, speaking in an unknown tongue, and someone else interpreting what was said, would have matched Paul's guidelines. Everyone speaking all at once does not.

Even though I was not unfamiliar with the gifts of the Spirit, and even though I knew the concept involved in what was being done, I did not feel comfortable with that service. To be frank, it seemed weird, and it did not bring glory to God in my mind. That is one man's opinion; actual mileage may vary.

Suppose I place myself in the shoes of a stranger to the Word, who had entered the service not knowing about gifts of the Spirit. Not knowing what to expect, I would most likely have thought it was madness, and I would have left, lest it be catching. It would not have made me want to turn towards Jesus; it would have made me want to run from all who speak His Name.

We know from the Bible that the Holy Spirit points to Jesus, and Jesus points to the Father. If something points us away from the Father, we may wish to rethink whether it is from the Holy Spirit at all.

There are two extremes we can cling to when it comes to spiritual gifts. One of them is to throw out the entire idea, and the other is to obsess over it. On the one hand, I have heard some Christians claim that the gifts of the Spirit were for the Apostolic age, and that we instead have the Bible as our guide. On the other hand, I have heard it claimed that if you are truly saved, you will speak in unknown tongues.

The truth is somewhere between the extremes. It's not an easy balance to find. We do not wish to quench the Spirit – to stand in the way of what God is doing – but at the same time we do not wish to say that we are acting by the Spirit, when the Spirit is really not in it. So how do we know if something is from the Spirit?

Prayer, and reading the Bible, to start with. Notice, for example, that Paul starts his treatise on spiritual gifts by telling us that they edify the entire church. He talks about us all being parts of one body, and tells us that the eye has a special gift that the hand does not, and vice versa. Neither part is better than the other: We would regret the loss of an eye as much as we would regret the loss of a hand.

Paul even goes on to point out that we have some parts we cover and hide, but even those parts are important. Some parts of the body are obvious and honorable, others less obvious (the gall bladder comes to mind) and even concealed. But the body is the sum of its parts, and not just a single part by itself.

So it is key to understanding the gifts of the Spirit that they don't glorify the individual who has the gift, but they lift up and glorify the entire church. The eye works to keep the entire body informed, and by its sight, the knee keeps from banging into chairs. The knee upholds the body, and moves it, eyes and all, from place to place. Each part builds up and works for the whole.

This is how the church should be, and this is how the gifts of the Spirit work together.

And having served us this example, then Paul shows us *"a more excellent way"* by dropping this bombshell:

> [1Co 13:1-3 NASB]
> *1 If I speak with the tongues of men and of angels, but do not have love, I have become a noisy gong or a clanging cymbal.*
> *2 If I have the gift of prophecy, and know all mysteries and all knowledge; and if I have all faith, so as to remove mountains, but do not have love, I am nothing.*

3 And if I give all my possessions to feed the poor, and if I surrender my body to be burned, but do not have love, it profits me nothing.

In essence, Paul is telling us that if we have wonderful supernatural gifts of God, but we use them without showing love, and without building up the whole church, we're not doing God's work. We're just beating on a trashcan with a stick.

The passage that follows this pronouncement is one of the most beautiful and profound poems ever written. It talks about the nature of Love, and what love is like. People recite this passage at their weddings; some have gone so far as to tattoo it onto their skin.

Then, and only then, having covered the place of spiritual gifts in the church (for its edification) and the key element in the use of gifts (open-handed love), Paul tells us to desire the gifts, and to desire to prophesy. (1 Cor. 14:1ff)

And then, having covered the manner by which the gifts are to be used, Paul concludes his treatise on the gifts (or at least in this particular instance) by calling for orderly use of the Spiritual gifts, telling us that:

1 Cor. 14:33 KJV
33 For God is not the author of confusion, but of peace, as in all churches of the saints.

and

1 Cor 14:40 KJV
40 Let all things be done decently and in order.

In thinking of spiritual gifts, we should also consider Romans 12, in which Paul talks about how to use those gifts that we are given through God's grace:

[Rom 12:3-8 NASB]
3 For through the grace given to me I say to everyone among you not to think more highly of himself than he ought to think; but to think so as to have sound

judgment, as God has allotted to each a measure of faith.

4 For just as we have many members in one body and all the members do not have the same function,

5 so we, who are many, are one body in Christ, and individually members one of another.

6 Since we have gifts that differ according to the grace given to us, [each of us is to exercise them accordingly:] if prophecy, according to the proportion of his faith;

7 if service, in his serving; or he who teaches, in his teaching;

8 or he who exhorts, in his exhortation; he who gives, with liberality; he who leads, with diligence; he who shows mercy, with cheerfulness.

You will notice, first, that Paul again starts by saying that we are one body, with many parts. He spells out, just prior, that the use of the gifts must be done in humility and sound judgment. You will also notice that the list of gifts here overlaps the list in 1 Cor 12-14, but is not an exact match. From this, we can conclude that the lists are not meant to be definitive. There are more gifts than are mentioned here.

Again, there is a ditch on each side of the road, and we must be careful not to fall into either. We might say that unless a person has one of the gifts enumerated in one of these passages, then he has no Spiritual gift, and this would be a mistake. We could also simply point to any natural talent and call it a spiritual gift, such as the gift of bottle washing, and this would be the opposite mistake. Paul calls us to sound judgment, so let us be guided first and foremost by our humility and our sound judgment.

The middle of the road – the balance point – is to look for ways that people use gifts in the church beyond their simple natural talents. Spiritual Gifts go beyond. They do not stop at a mere talent; they reach into the realm of the remarkable, the noteworthy, and the awe-inspiring.

Not everyone likes to talk about the spiritual gifts, and that is understandable. Those who are inclined to ridicule the church are quick to point to abuses – so-called faith healers who have been shown to be frauds; so-called prophets using radio transmitters. So long as there has been a church, there have been people abusing the practices of the church. Even in the book of Acts, Luke tells of a man named Simon who tried to buy the Holy Spirit from Paul. He apparently thought that giving the gifts of the Spirit was a magic trick, and had a secret method that he might use to make money. Sadly, it even appears that he was a believer – a Christian! – And still thought in such worldly terms.

Did I mention that Christians are merely sinners, saved by God's grace?

Spiritual Gifts are not the only thing that trouble Christians. Another rabbit hole is to try to answer every critic of Christianity. If the truth were told, that is a rabbit hole in which I often find myself. One thing that I have learned is that we cannot answer every criticism of Christianity for one simple reason: The Critics of Christianity don't want to hear it.

Not every non-Christian falls into this category, but the folks who are most adamant in criticizing Christianity will seldom listen to the reasonable viewpoint. It is easy to snap out a seemingly clever question, such as, "If God is omnipotent, could He make a rock so large that He couldn't lift it?"

It takes a willingness to think it through logically in order to understand that this is an improper question, that is, a question that assumes two contradictory things. It assumes that God is omnipotent, and then it assumes that there might exist a rock that is too big for an omnipotent being to lift it. Those two assumptions are mutually contradictory, so the question is improper.

Simply put, scoffing is easier than thinking.

There are also questions that arise concerning the last days. Many young Christians dive headlong into the book of Revelation and come out badly puzzled. Revelation is an important book, and has many important messages for the church, but it should not be the starting point on your study of the Bible. Nonetheless, the last days are not something we should ignore, either.

There are several places where the last days are talked about. One such place is Matthew 24, where the disciples ask Jesus about the time when the temple will be destroyed, and when the last days will come. Those are two separate questions, but the disciples could not imagine that the temple could be torn down without the world coming to an end as well. There is a lesson in that...

But Jesus did not stop them and separate the questions. He answered them as if it were one question, and gave a response that blends the two answers. One example of this double answer is in 24:15, where Jesus speaks of the Abomination of Desolation standing in the holy place.

The Abomination of Desolation – or the blasphemy which destroys everything – has already happened once, in the Jewish wars. There is some debate as to whether it occurred when a statue of a Roman Emperor was erected in the Most Holy Place, or as a result of later Roman pagan temples placed nearby. In any event, the blasphemy – The temple of God desecrated by a pagan statue – led to the rebellions and wars that raged from 66 AD to 70 AD, when the second temple was destroyed.

But because of the way Jesus spoke of it, many Christians anticipate a similar desecration that will signal the last phase of the end of days. So Jesus may have been speaking not of one future event, but of two. Jesus cites Daniel in this passage, and we can read more of the Abomination of Desolation in the book of Daniel, which preceded Jesus' birth by about 500 years or more.

This blended reference leads us to believe that Matthew 24 was both a prediction of the destruction of the second temple and a destruction of the third temple, which has not yet been built. Incidentally, the references to the destruction of the temple, in 70 AD, is one of the factors that leads skeptics to date Matthew's gospel much later than the given date in the fifties AD.

But this argument begs the question. It denies that Jesus predicted the destruction of the temple by saying that it must have been written after the Jewish wars because otherwise Jesus would be predicting the destruction of the temple. In other words, it is nothing more than an argument from incredulity.

In reading Matthew 24, we must also take note of verse 34, in which Jesus says that this will happen during the present generation. And in fact, the destruction of the temple occurred 37 years after He died – while the present generation was still alive. One can see this as a fulfilled prophecy, or as a sign that Matthew was written later than 70 AD, but the latter position, again, is due to fallacious reasoning.

Finally, take note of v. 36, which is probably the most important thing for us to take away from this chapter. Jesus states:

> *"But about that day or hour no one knows, not even the angels in heaven, nor the Son, but only the Father." (NIV)*

When you hear that Jesus will return upon a certain day, at a certain time, you need to immediately hear alarm bells. Jesus stated explicitly that no one knows the day nor the hour. Anyone who says that he knows when Jesus will return is mistaken.

Jesus goes on to tell the disciples that because they cannot be certain when He will return, they need to be busy doing His work. He wishes to come to them suddenly and find that they have been using their time wisely, and though surprised by His coming, they have nothing to fear.

Avoid any so-called prophet who tells you a certain day when Jesus will return. Do not follow such a teacher.

Next, the end times are talked about in Thessalonians 4, where the Apostle Paul says this:

> (1Thess. 4:13-16 NIV)
> *13 Brothers and sisters, we do not want you to be uninformed about those who sleep in death, so that you do not grieve like the rest of mankind, who have no hope.*
> *14 For we believe that Jesus died and rose again, and so we believe that God will bring with Jesus those who have fallen asleep in him.*
> *15 According to the Lord's word, we tell you that we who are still alive, who are left until the coming of the Lord, will certainly not precede those who have fallen asleep.*
> *16 For the Lord himself will come down from heaven, with a loud command, with the voice of the archangel and with the trumpet call of God, and the dead in Christ will rise first.*

17 After that, we who are still alive and are left will be caught up together with them in the clouds to meet the Lord in the air. And so we will be with the Lord forever.

Here, Paul gives us a snapshot of the return of Christ, with the dead saints rising to meet Him in the air, and then those of us who are alive and remain will join them.

And at least one reader is wondering how that will work. Well, Paul gives us another snapshot in 1 Cor. 15, where he says,

(1 Cor. 15:50-55 NIV)
50 I declare to you, brothers and sisters, that flesh and blood cannot inherit the kingdom of God, nor does the perishable inherit the imperishable.
51 Listen, I tell you a mystery: We will not all sleep, but we will all be changed—
52 in a flash, in the twinkling of an eye, at the last trumpet. For the trumpet will sound, the dead will be raised imperishable, and we will be changed.
53 For the perishable must clothe itself with the imperishable, and the mortal with immortality.
54 When the perishable has been clothed with the imperishable, and the mortal with immortality, then the saying that is written will come true: "Death has been swallowed up in victory."
55 "Where, O death, is your victory? Where, O death, is your sting?"

The quotation in vv. 54-55 comes from the Old Testament prophet, Hosea. In the middle of a passage warning about the coming Assyrian Captivity, he suddenly declares in the Name of the Lord that God will redeem His people from death and the grave. And through Jesus He has done that.

But we see from vv. 50-54 that an important change must occur in the nature of our bodies. We don't know all of the details of that change. But we do have one Example from which we can try to form a good guess: Jesus Himself.

After the resurrection, Jesus had a visible corporeal form. He ate bread and fish among the disciples; He challenged Thomas to touch Him and see that He is real. At the same time, His body was different. He was able to materialize among the disciples in a locked room. He was able to rise up into the air, and disappear into the clouds. And yet He sat on the beach at Galilee, made a fire with sticks, and baked fish for the disciples' breakfast.

So we can reasonably suppose that our bodies after this transformation will be similar to our bodies before, and yet very different; useful, but no longer limited.

Other references to the end times are mostly found in two prophetic books, and both of them use an unusual style of writing known as the apocalyptic style. The powerful images and exotic descriptions are not easy to interpret.

These books are the second half of the book of Daniel, and the book of Revelation. But before I send you into these, looking for the exact sequence of events leading to the end of days, I must warn you that there are many pitfalls as well. Be careful that you consider the visions carefully. Do not latch onto a single interpretation and assume that it is the only way to understand that particular passage. I urge you to use reliable and time-tested guides, such as Matthew Henry's commentary.

Do not rely on this popular writer or that one; instead look for a balanced and well-grounded approach that incorporates the entire passage. Verses out of context are the accuser's playthings.

Part of the accuser's game – and the accuser always has a game – is to make us concentrate on one thing, as if that one thing were the entire sum of all our Christian duties. Eschatology – the study of last things – is one of those places where we can easily become consumed and miss the point.

Would it be a really good thing to decode the name of the beast, and to recognize him when he arose to power? Sure. But it is thousands of times more important that when Jesus returns, he finds us at work, doing what He told us to do. And Jesus says so in Matthew 24. This is not a difference between good and evil, and that is why it makes a stumbling block for us. It is instead a difference between a good but less important thing, and a better and more important thing.

So what is the most important thing that Jesus told us to do? I'm glad you asked.

> [Mat 28:18-20 NASB]
> *18 And Jesus came up and spoke to them, saying, "All authority has been given to Me in heaven and on earth.*
> *19 "Go therefore and make disciples of all the nations, baptizing them in the name of the Father and the Son and the Holy Spirit,*
> *20 teaching them to observe all that I commanded you; and lo, I am with you always, even to the end of the age."*

So, let's see: going to the ends of the Earth, making disciples, baptizing them in the name of the Father, and of the Son, and of the Holy Spirit, and teaching them to observe all of the commands that Jesus gave us... Those would be the things that are more important than going down a doctrinal rabbit hole.

I'm not saying that doctrine is not important. It is critical that we keep a close eye on our doctrine. What we teach needs to be in line with what Jesus taught. But the most important things are listed in the great commands and the great commission.

You remember the great commands, I'm sure. Love the LORD your God with all your heart, and all your soul, and all your mind, and with all your strength; and the second is like the first: Love your neighbor as yourself. The great commission is the passage above, in which we are ordered to go and share the gospel of Jesus Christ. These things take precedence – must take precedence – over things like figuring out who shall be Pendragon of Logres in the age when Glund shall descend.

There are other rabbit holes we can go down besides eschatology, such as figuring out what will happen to those who have never had a chance to hear the gospel. There may be a biblical answer to that question... In pondering it, I go back and forth between Romans 1:20 and Acts 17:31. But in the end, we can be confident that God will be fair, whatever He chooses to do.

We can go down the rabbit hole of whether we chose God or He chose us – personally, it seems to me that it's a bit of both. One pastor remarked that when we approach heaven's gate from the outside, we will see the words across the arch: "Whosoever will may come" (Acts 2:21; Rev. 22:17). But when we look back at the gate from within, we will see the words "I chose you before the foundation of the world" (Eph. 1:4).

So how do we, as Christians, avoid going down the rabbit holes or being trampled by the elephants? Well, as Paul told us in Romans 12:2, we keep renewing our minds. And how do we renew our minds? By reading the Bible and through prayer.

Remember how we talked in Stage 1 about the principal disciplines of a Christian? Well, here we've come full circle, and we're back to the beginning: It all hinges on reading and praying over the Bible. It's all about letting the Spirit of God breath new life into us through the Word and through communion with God.

Another Digression: On the Diet of Worms

We mentioned in a prior chapter that a diet is one type of religious conference, and that there was one held in the city of Worms, Germany, in the year 1521. This particular diet was held to figure out what the Roman Catholic Church should do about the teachings of Martin Luther, who started the Protestant Reform.

There are a lot of things we could say about the Diet of Worms, and most of them would be peripheral at best to the actual practice of Christianity. So let's instead consider a different kind of a diet of worms.

We all recall the childhood lament, *Nobody likes me, everybody hates me, gonna go eat some worms*. It is a parody of the sort of self-pity that children sometimes exhibit. But at the same time, there is a similar form of self-pity that creeps into the church. People become offended over very minor slights, some of them so small that we would shrug them off if they happened on the street, or even in the workplace. But how dare someone treat me like that, in the House of God! Did you hear what he said?

There's a joke about a man stranded on a deserted island, who was rescued by a ship after ten years alone. As he showed the ship's crew how he lived for those ten years, they asked about the three huts that they saw on the beach. The castaway explained that the first hut was his home, where he slept. The second hut was his church, where he would go on Sunday to commune with God and to think about scripture.

When the crew asked about the third hut, the man made a face. "Oh," he said, "That's the church that I *used* to attend."

While humorous in this light – the man could not even stay in fellowship with himself, let alone others – it is illustrative of the offense we take over meaningless injuries. The church is not a place for our pride; it is a place for communing with God and other Christians through prayer and the reading of the word.

It doesn't seem to occur to us that we are not the ones who should be offended by a slight in the house of God. It is for God to be offended, or no one at all.

Don't get me wrong: I'm not advocating for us to be rude in church. I'm simply asking that we treat churches as hospitals for sinners, some of whom will offend us in various ways. Let's consider the source of the slight, and forgive each other, instead of, well, eating worms... metaphorically or literally.

Practical actions to take, when someone says or does something in church that you don't like, might include:

1. Forgiving them. Consciously forgive them, right then.
2. Praying for them. A quick word to God, on that person's behalf, right at that moment... What could it hurt?
3. Asking ourselves if we are doing or saying things for which others need to forgive us.
4. Smiling politely, or better still, with genuine Christian love.

It will go far in our Christian maturity if we guard ourselves against being easily offended. Let's all do our best to avoid the diet of worms. Please, don't be a vermivore.

STAGE NINE
Remaining Faithful

SO, WE'VE PRAYED, and we've read the Bible until we seem to know it backwards. We're working to do justice, love mercy, and walk humbly with our God. What do we do now?

Paul gives us an instruction in Romans 12: 1-1:

1 Therefore I urge you, brethren, by the mercies of God, to present your bodies a living and holy sacrifice, acceptable to God, which is your spiritual service of worship.
2 And do not be conformed to this world, but be transformed by the renewing of your mind, so that you may prove what the will of God is, that which is good and acceptable and perfect.

That's a tall order. Paul wants us to be a living sacrifice, that is, wholly devoted to God, as if we had been burned up on an altar, and yet alive and working to edify the church, through our daily devotion and worship. On top of that, we are not to become like the world, but we are to keep renewing our minds, to be like Christ instead – proving, or finding out, what God wants from us (His will) and demonstrating that it is good, acceptable, and perfect.

It's overwhelming.

It's like when I couldn't conceive of how I, one sailor, was expected to fight engine room fires – and the answer was that I was to follow through with a series of pre-planned, well-organized tasks, which would all mesh together into the overall plan.

So what's the overall plan for us to become Living Sacrifices?

Well, we continue growing in the faith. Have I mentioned reading the Bible and praying?

In addition to those foundation stones, there are many books that you might read to help you learn and grow – nearly anything you can find by C.S. Lewis or by G. K. Chesterton is worth its weight in gold for Christian growth.

You might consider formal education in Christian Studies, perhaps at a Bible College. You might consider seminary training. Or you might simply continue to study the Word and to pray. There will never come a time in your life when you have mastered Christianity, and can stop reading the Bible and praying.

God had a powerful servant in Billy Graham, the great evangelist. Graham lived a long and fruitful life filled with the power of God. He preached to hundreds of thousands, including presidents. His careful protection of his relationship with God is a shining example of Christian integrity.

I remember seeing him interviewed on television once, after he was a very old man. The interviewer asked, "When you get to heaven, and you see God, what do you hope He will say to you?"

Graham responded, " 'Well done, thou good and faithful servant,' … But I don't think that's what He'll say."

So even Billy Graham, the paragon of Godly Christian living, was not satisfied that he was ready to meet God… Not even after all of the great things that he had done and the multitudes he had led into the Kingdom of God. And that makes me believe that none of us are really ever finished as Christians, until we draw that last breath and step into the Divine presence. And even then, we will need to be covered by God's grace.

In considering how even a great saint of God did not feel prepared, I had to wonder if perhaps we have no real idea of what yardstick God applies, in looking at our lives. Remember the widow who gave the tiny coin: To Jesus, that coin was worth more than the great wealth that the rich gave.

I wonder if there will some, on the last day, who discover that their work, a seeming failure on earth, was a great victory in God's eye. I imagine perhaps a pastor who weeps that in his long ministry, not one person converted to Christianity; I see God saying to him, "I did not send you to convert them. That is My job. I only sent you to minister to them, and in that you were faithful."

But be that as it may, we remain imperfect. As Paul tells us in 2 Corinthians, we have this treasure – the very Spirit of God! – and we carry it around in clay vessels, that is, these bodies we inhabit. We have holiness housed in dirt.

How then shall we go on as Christians? What do we need to do in order to eventually be perfect?

Continue. Live for God day by day. Live each day more fully than the day before. Draw closer to God through the Bible and prayer. Day by day, one day at a time.

And take to heart Paul's instructions from Philippians 4:8:

> *Finally, brothers, whatever is true, whatever is honorable, whatever is just, whatever is pure, whatever is lovely, whatever is commendable, if there is any excellence, if there is anything worthy of praise, think about these things.*

I wish you the best in your walk with God. I pray that He will bless and guide you, day by day. And on the last day, I will see you in the New Jerusalem.

Godspeed.

Appendices

Glossary
Appendix A: A Parable as an Overview of World Religions.
Appendix B: A Brief Outline of the Bible.
Appendix C: A Quick Survey of the Books of the Bible
Appendix D: The Pre-Pauline Doctrine, the Apostles' Creed, and the Nicene Creed
Appendix E: The Romans Road, with Examples of Salvation Recorded in the New Testament.
Recommended Reading

GLOSSARY

THESE ARE THE meaning of words and phrases as they are used in this book. You may find different meanings expressed in other Lexicons, but this is how these words and phrases are used in this book.

Assert, Assertion – (To make) A firm declaration which is not yet proven. "But whom Paul asserts to be alive." Acts 26:19

Apochrypha – Literally, "the hidden, or the secret." The "hidden secret" part refers to the provenance of "apochryphal" works, thus the meaning is closer to "uncertain." In theology, the section of the Bible that lies between the Old and New Testaments, and that Protestant and Non-conformist Christians do not accept as canonical.

Apologetics – From the Greek word Apologia, meaning defense, Apologetics is the verbal defense of an idea or argument. In Ancient Greece, an apologia was a defense presented in court when one was accused of a crime. Christian apologetics is the defense of the Christian faith.

Argument by Desire – A proof offered by C. S. Lewis to the effect that just as a human's thirst implies that he is a creature that naturally drinks water, so our desire for the Divine is evidence that we were made for fellowship with God.

Arminianism – the belief that salvation comes by a Free Will choice.

Atonement – To reconcile by correcting an offense; to bring together; to make two people "At One" or as one. Jesus' act of Atonement sets us at one with God.

A. W. Tozer – Christian theologian; author of The Pursuit of God.

Calvinism – The belief that salvation is predestined.

Consequences – The natural results – usually bad – of an action. The consequences of sin are death and hell.

C.S. Lewis – Clive Staples "Jack" Lewis, b. 1898, d. 1963; Cambridge Professor, author of The Screwtape Letters, Mere Christianity, God in the Dock, A Pilgrim's Regress, the Abolition of Man, The Great Divorce, and many other books. Although not Lewis' primary field of study, he is best known for his theological works, all of which are excellent for apologetic studies.

Denomination – one of many divisions of Christianity, most of which agree in most of their beliefs. Roman Catholicism, the Southern Baptist Convention, Lutheranism and Methodism are all denominations.

Discernment – The ability to notice differences in the thoughts and intents of people, or to judge good and evil. Discernment may be simple wisdom, or may be a spiritual gift. It may be manifested in logic and argument, or as a word of knowledge or wisdom.

Discipline – The process of studying, or of being a disciple; to undergo a course of study; the course of study itself.

Edify, Edification – Edify means "to build up." An edifice is a building. Edification means the process of building up, especially building the mind or spirit of a person or persons, as, "For the edification of the church."

Essential – Pertaining to the essence of something. Or, a part of the essence of, and thus crucial to, something.

Etymology – The way that a word developed; the roots from which the word was formed. This often gives insight into the word itself, and what it means.

Everlasting Man, the – A book by G.K. Chesterton, exploring two main premises: That mankind is unique among the animals, and that Jesus of Nazareth was unique among men. Chesterton also points out most atheists today are not truly outside the church, but are merely spoiled Christians, who must either draw closer to, or move farther from the church, in order to judge her objectively.

Exegesis – The process of drawing out a meaning from a text. We must always be careful to use proper rules when drawing out a meaning, so that we do not insert a meaning into the text.

Filial Piety – Respect and Reverence for, and one's duties towards, one's family, and especially one's parents. Friendship may also be considered a form of filial piety (a friend as a figurative brother).

G. K. Chesterton – Early 20th century writer; author of "The Everlasting Man," a book that strongly argues in support of the Christian Faith. If you can find it, read it.

Gameliel – A famous rabbi of the first century BC / First century AD; a teacher of Saul of Tarsus, who was later called Paul the Apostle.

Grace – Grace is something that we receive but do not deserve. God gives us His Grace by giving us the gift of eternal life with

Him (Romans 6:23). We don't deserve it. He graciously gives it anyway.

Hamartology – Teachings about sin, how sin affects us, why we sin, and how to avoid and overcome sin.

Humility, Humble, Humbly – The opposite of harmful pride. When we recognize that others are worthy individuals for whom Christ died, and treat them accordingly, we exercise humility.

Ichthys, "**IXOYE**" – A Greek acronym for the Greek words that mean "Jesus Christ, God's Son, Savior." The word "Ichthys" is Greek for "Fish," so you may see the word associated with a crude sketch of a fish.

Iniquity – One of two categories of sin mentioned in the Bible. Iniquity is to "miss the mark" or to fall short of a goal. See also, transgression.

Intangible – Not able to be touched. Love, happiness, thoughts, and the human soul are all intangible.

Invitation, Altar Call – A part of an evangelical worship service in which congregants are invited to come to the altar and make decisions, such as a profession of faith, or to join the church. One may also come to the altar to pray, or to request prayer by the pastor.

Irrelevant – Not related to the topic at hand, immaterial, not pertinent, beside the point, moot.

Irreverent – Not respectful. God deserves our reverence; Sophists and most so-called Philosophers do not.

Jesus of Nazareth, Jesus Christ, Jesus the Messiah – An historical man who lived from about 1 BC to about 33 AD. He worked miracles, and called Himself the Messiah (see John 4:26, for example). Messiah, or "anointed one," was the name used by the Jews for a divine King who was to come, based on ancient prophecies (compare, for example, Psalm 22 (circa 1000 BC) and Isaiah 53 (circa 500 BC) with the crucifixion of Christ in the gospels). Christ is the Latin word meaning "Anointed," and is usually applied to Jesus, as a title. Jesus died for the sins of mankind and rose again on the third day.

John – Two men of this name appear significantly in the life of Christ: John the Baptist (second cousin of Jesus; his mother Elisabeth was Mary's cousin) and John the Disciple, who wrote the New Testament books of John (also called the Gospel of John), 1 John, 2 John, 3 John (letters), and the Revelation of John (also called Revelation). John the Disciple was the second most prolific of New Testament writers. Bible novices sometimes confuse John the Baptist with John the Disciple.

Justice – Doing what is right. In the Biblical sense, it means to treat others fairly and to refrain from cheating them. There is also the philosophical concept of Perfect Justice, which writers such as Camus, Kafka, and others claim is unobtainable in this life. C. S. Lewis uses the desire for Perfect Justice, couple with its unavailable nature, to suggest that we were designed for a different life.

Justified – Made just, or reconciled with Justice. My sin is justified by Jesus' sacrifice, and it is "Just-if-I'd" never sinned (Okay, that should be "Just-as-if-I'd," but that doesn't fit the pun).

Law of Grace – In Paul's letter to the Romans, he talks about how the moral laws outlined in the Old Testament were mainly intended to show us that we were not capable of being moral; All have sinned and fall short of the glory of God. Paul then shows us a better way to live, having been forgiven by Christ: The Law of Grace, which is to say, obedience to God based not on fear of punishment or the following of obscure rules for those rules' own sake, but on our love for Christ, who loved us first. A powerful love, such as the redeeming blood of Jesus, demands that we answer with our best and highest love in return, and this is the Law of Grace.

Matthew Henry – An 18th century clergyman and theologian. Henry's Commentary on the Whole Bible is widely considered the best Protestant/Non-conformist commentary.

Meaning of Life – The philosophical purpose for which human life exists; the highest Good; the Summum Bonum; the purpose; the reason; the only thing that's not striving after the wind. (hint: It's serving God.)

Mercy – When we deserve something bad, but don't get it, we have tasted Mercy. Mercy goes together with Grace. In Romans 6:23 we learn that the wages of sin is death, but that the Gift of God is Eternal life with Him through Jesus' sacrifice for us. That we don't get spiritual death is God's Mercy; that we can spend eternity with God is God's Grace.

Metaphor – A stylistic device used to explain a difficult idea by comparing it to something else. If we say, "The general stood like a rock," we are using the firmness of a rock (which everyone

understands) to explain the General's bravery under enemy fire (which may not be easily understood by those who did not see it).
Morals, Morality – Morality literally means a following of rules. The idea is that our society has adopted certain rules by which people ought to behave, and those who follow those rules are moral; those who defy them are immoral. Typically, social "mores" involve following the Ten Commandments and maintaining sobriety. People sometimes assume that Jesus taught people to be moral, but in fact Jesus showed the flaws of first-century morality, and called for people to obey a higher law – the Law of Grace.
Nicodemus – A Jewish leader and a member of the Sanhedrin, who became a secret follower of Jesus. See John 3. Also, one of two men who acquired Jesus body after the crucifixion, to bury it.
Non-conformist – Someone who doesn't fit the pattern. In Christianity, a Non-conformist is someone who does not conform to a certain creed, especially someone who is neither Catholic nor Protestant. Technically, Protestant denominations are a reformation of the Roman Catholic Church, but there are some denominations which were never part of it, and thus could not reform from it. These are best referred to as "Non-conformists." Piedmontese, Anabaptists, and others tend to claim a non-conformist heritage.
Novice – Someone who is new to something, especially a religious order or religious studies.
Paul E. Little –– Author of *Know What You Believe*, a guide to Christian doctrines of various denominations.
Paul the Apostle – A former student of Gamaliel, and a fervent defender of Judaism against the encroachment of Christianity, later a convert and eventually an apostle of Christ. Paul was the first Christian missionary, and wrote most of the New Testament.
Piety – Reverence, respect, or obligation for God or for one's family. In Plato's Euthyphro, Socrates confronts Euthyphro for failing in his Filial Piety (Reverence towards his family).
Prayer – A conversation with God. Prayer can be formal, informal, long, short, calm, or passionate. Whichever it is, God would like to hear from you. Today, if that fits your schedule.
Prescribe – To recommend or order, especially as a cure or remedy.
Prodigal – Having turned away from the truth or from moral good. Typically used in reference to Jesus' parable of the prodigal son,

who was gladly received back by his father, when he repented and returned home.

Profession of Faith – A public statement declaring that one has faith in Jesus Christ. See Romans 10:9-10; compare Peter's spontaneous statement in Matthew 16:16.

Proscribe – To forbid or to order something not to be done.

Pseudonym – An assumed name or "nom-de-plume."

Question – A query, or a matter under debate. "To be or not to be, that is the question…" (Shakespeare, Hamlet).

Reconcile – To bring facts into harmony; to resolve a difference or to settle an argument. The word suggests accounting and bookkeeping; settling the accounts; it can also be used with regard to the restoration of a relationship.

Redeem – To buy back, or to retrieve from a state of forfeiture. In the Old Testament, family members were permitted to buy back lost property every seventh year. The book of Ruth hinges upon redemption by a Kinsman. This is a symbol – a "type"—of how Jesus redeems us from our sin.

Relevant – Having to do with the matter being discussed, pertinent, apropos, on the topic.

Reverent – Respectful. God deserves reverence.

Revelation – A fact or event revealed by God to a person. Also, the name of a book written by John the Disciple, a/k/a John the Revelator, a/k/a John the Elder.

Righteousness – The state of being morally and ethically right. As a human pursuit, it is unattainable, but it is given freely by God to those who hunger and thirst for it.

Roman Road – A set of Bible verses, all from the book of Romans, which lead to personal salvation. Romans 3:23, Romans 6:23, Romans 5:8, and Romans 10:9 provide a basic step-by-step plan of salvation: All have sinned; sin leads to death (hell); God loves us despite our sin; and if we confess Jesus as our Lord, believing that God raised Him from the dead, we can be saved from the penalty of our sins.

Salvation – Being saved. In this context, being saved from the penalty of our own sins.

Sanctification – The process by which believers are made Holy, over time, as they learn to defeat the power of sin in their lives.

Sect of the Way – An early description of Christianity, which was initially considered a strange sect of Judaism. It draws its name from the fact that Jesus called Himself "The Way, the Truth, and the Life" (John 14:6)

Security of the Believer – The doctrine that salvation establishes a permanent and unbreakable relationship with God.

Sin – Doing what is wrong in the eyes of God.

Sincere – Without deception, sarcasm, or hidden intention; honest.

Soteriology – Teachings about salvation: Why we need to be saved, how we are saved, what it means to be saved from the consequences of our sins.

Supernatural – Literally, "More than natural" or "Above the natural." Spiritual matters are "Supernatural" to the human mind; though one imagines that they are simply "Natural" to God, who created nature.

Synagogue – A building used for weekly worship by the Hebrew people. This worship typically involves readings from the TaNaKh, and especially the Torah.

Tabernacle – A tent used for religious meetings, especially for the purpose of being in the presence of God, most especially that tent carried by the Israelites during the exodus from Egypt, above which God was present in the form of a pillar of cloud and of fire. A parallel is drawn in John 1:14, in which we are told that Jesus "dwelt" among us (literally "pitched His tent among us"). This metaphor is intended to parallel the physical presence of Jesus with the presence of God above the tabernacle of meeting, in the wilderness.

Tanakh – A Hebrew acronym and abbreviation meaning, "The Law, the Prophets, and the Writings." These are the books that Christians refer to as the Old Testament. One might also refer to it as the "Old Covenant."

Tangible – Capable of being touched, sensible, physical.

Temple, The – One of three buildings through the course of Hebrew History, built upon the site designated by God. These are: Solomon's Temple (ca. 1000 BC to ca. 500 BC); Nehemiah's Temple (also called Herod's Temple, due to Herod's renovations) (ca. 420 BC – 69 AD); and a future temple to be built in the end times, on the same site.

Testimony – A statement of facts known to the one who testifies; The statement of a witness to an event or a fact. In a religious context, the explanation of one's life before Christ, one's own direct interactions with Christ, and one's life after meeting Christ. It is sometimes misused in certain circles to mean an irrational assurance of things that one cannot directly know, based upon a "burning in the bosom" feeling.

Theology – From the Greek words Theos and Logos, literally "Words about God." Theology in its broad scope is the study of all religion; in the intermediate scope, the study of Christianity, and in its narrow scope, the study of the Christian God. Theology in the intermediate scope includes Theology Proper (study of God the Father), Christology (study of Christ), Pneumatology (study of the Holy Spirit), Angelology (study of angels), Soteriology (study of salvation), Hamartology (study of sin) and Eschatology (study of last things).

Torah, the – The first five books of the Bible, also called the books of Moses, or the books of the Law.

Transgressions – One of two categories of sins mentioned in the Bible. Transgression means a crossing of a line or the violation of a boundary. See also, Iniquity. Transgression can also imply the betrayal of one to whom you had an obligation or trust. To steal is a transgression, to steal from a neighbor doubly so.

Universalism – The belief that everyone will eventually get into heaven, regardless of whether or not they were Christians. This belief is not supported by Scripture.

Woman at the Well – A woman mentioned, but not named, who encountered Jesus at a well in Samaria. See John 4. Of particular note in this passage is the moral imperative in 4:1 (Jesus "must needs" pass through Samaria), the persistence of Jesus in bringing the conversation to spiritual things, the statement about God in 4:24, and Jesus' confession of Deity in 4:26.

Yeshua, Y'shua HaMaschiah – Hebrew name of Jesus, Jesus the Messiah.

Zeitgeist – Literally, the "Spirit of the Age." Zeitgeist is usually used to refer to the currently fashionable concept.

80 Eridani – A star that is between 5 and 7 light-years from Earth. Also the star most similar to the Star Trek star "Vulcan."

Appendix A:
A Parable as an Overview of World Religions.

This parable was first recited to me by a man named Woodrow Knight. He stated that he did not know the original source,* but that it had been recited to him by another man, and so forth, down several generations of teachings. I have taken the liberty of modifying it slightly over the years, to include more information, and to improve accuracy.

The purpose of this parable is to teach a comparison of a single point, namely the hamartology and soteriology (sin and salvation teachings) of the various religions mentioned. It is not an all-inclusive textbook, nor is it entirely fair to those religions. On the other hand, nothing in my studies has led me to find this analogy grossly inaccurate, aside from its summary format.

A certain man was walking in a field of tall grasses when he suddenly fell into a hidden pit. He was unhurt by his fall, and as his eyes adjusted to the darkness, he found himself in an abandoned cistern. The walls were to smooth and too damp to climb.

On one wall of the cistern, there were metal rungs driven into the stone. If he were to leap, he could catch the lowest and might pull himself out of the pit. But wrapped around the lowest rung was a deadly viper, of a particularly venomous sort. If he touched the rung, he would die at once.

He began to shout.

KRSHNA was passing by, and looked down into the pit, where he saw the man.

"Take joy," he said. "For the pit is an illusion. The viper may kill you, but this too is an illusion. You will live again, and if you do good works, perhaps you may fall into a pit that is less deep." **

KRSHNA then continued on his way, leaving the man in the pit. In time, BUDDHA passed by.

"I see that you are in a pit," said BUDDHA. "I see that you are very unhappy, because you wish to be out of the pit. The solution is very simple. Stop wishing to be out of the pit, and you can be happy." ***

Then BUDDHA also went along his way.

LAO TZE *was passing by, and looked into the pit. "Ah," he said. "So it was your nature to be in a pit. Accept the nature with which you have been born, and draw strength from it."* LAO TZE *also continued along his way.*

MOHAMMED *was passing near and looked down into the pit. "You should not have fallen into the pit," he said. "Allah does not look with favor upon those who fall into pits." He shook his head and left.*

MOSES *was passing by. He looked down into the pit and was moved with compassion. "You will need strength so that you do not perish, waiting for your Rescuer," said* MOSES, *and he lowered bread and wine into the well, so that the man could eat. Then* MOSES *hurried away to find...* ****

JESUS, *who came running to the well. He leaped down beside the man, raised him onto His shoulders, and carried him up the rungs, setting him at last on the firm ground.* JESUS *accepted the serpent's bite but looked upon it with disdain, even though it took His life.*

I am that man. The pit is my sin. The serpent is death. JESUS *took the death that I deserved so that He might lift me out of the trap that my own sin had made.*

As we said earlier, this is an analogy and a metaphor. It is not a complete recitation of the relative sin and salvation teachings of the religions mentioned. But it does summarize them.

Hinduism (represented by KRSHNA) does teach that this present world is illusory. I had one former Hindu object to this characterization, stating first that only a minority of Hindus believe reality to be an illusion. He also stated that KRSHNA and BUDDHA would have taught the man, collectively, over many karmic cycles, to kill the serpent, make a rope of its skin, and thus raise himself from the pit.

Hinduism and Buddhism both teach that the dead are reincarnated, and are raised or lowered in their stations according to their karma (a "bank balance" of good or evil done in former lives). Thus going through many karmic cycles means allowing the serpent to kill the man, over and over. This is why KRSHNA says that perhaps he may fall into a pit that is less deep, that is, replace his bad karma with better karma and thus be less in debt to sin.

Buddhism also teaches that the karmic cycles needed (i.e. deaths and rebirths) can be reduced through changes in one's outlook on life. Thus BUDDHA advises the man to stop wanting out of the pit, so that he can be happy.

Taoism is represented by LAO TZE, its founder. Taoism teaches that each living creature has a taproot (or "Tao") from which it draws negative and positive energies. The balance of these energies (Yin and Yang) causes good health, good fortune, and good deeds, while an imbalance causes sickness, poverty, and evil.

LAO TZE famously said, in a conversation with Confucius, that the swan does not need a daily washing to remain white, nor the raven an inking to remain black. By implication, this would mean that their fundamental natures – the "flow of energy within them" – cannot be changed. One can only accept one's nature as it is. Thus, he tells the man that to be in the pit is the man's nature.

MOHAMMED can offer no concrete advice for the remission of sins. He can only rebuke the man for having sinned.

MOSES has a practical response, even if it is incomplete. The bread and wine represent the system of sacrifices offered in the temple for the remission of sin, covering them or blotting them out. It is not sufficient to erase them altogether. For this, MOSES must call upon…

JESUS. It is JESUS, and only JESUS, who puts Himself into the same state as the man who is to be rescued. He accepts the death that the man deserves, and raises the man out of the pit by atoning for his sins.

While not a perfect exposition of all teachings on sin in all religions, this parable does offer a simplified view of those teachings.

The point of the parable – and it does have one – is that certain concepts are unique to Christianity. First, only Christianity teaches that escaping the effects of my sin is not something that I can do, and that therefore God Himself, in the person of Jesus Christ, did this for me.

Second, only Christianity teaches that we can get out of the pit in this life. Pantheism, such as Hinduism or Buddhism, would have us die many times in our sinful state before ascending to mastery and becoming one with the universe. Islam would have us die hoping that our sins were outweighed by our pious actions. Taoism offers no chance of correcting past mistakes. Judaism teaches the remission of sins through the ongoing sacrifices of innocent animals.

Christianity alone teaches that God Himself made one perfect sacrifice forever, rescuing us from our sins, now and until we meet Him on the last day.

---

* As a side note: One of my friends, Dr. Jean-Paul G. Potet, has brought to my attention a similar tale of pulling a man from a pit, related in an ancient Hindu book of wisdom, the Panchatantra. In that tale, a man pulls four beings from a pit; a monkey, a tiger, a serpent, and a man.

Each promises a reward to the rescuer. In time, the rescuer visits each of the creatures, and each treats him faithfully, except for the man, who frames him for murder. The serpent aids the rescuer in obtaining his freedom and exacting revenge. The moral lesson in the Panchatantra is that one must pay one's debts faithfully, and that one must be wary of promises, especially those given in desperation. It is unrelated to our parable here.

The Panchatantra can be thought of as a source for Aesop's Fables, and follows a similar pattern of brief vignettes with anthropomorphized animals, each ending with a moral lesson. It is not a holy book of any kind, and it should not be viewed as scripture.

** Hinduism and Buddhism teach that a person is re-incarnated many times, and through good karma (an accumulated balance of good deeds) may rise to a higher station in the next life. Each living being, they reason, is somewhere along this chain, with some creatures rising because of good karma, and others falling because of bad karma. After many uncountable cycles of lives, they teach that one may eventually achieve a state known as Nirvana, in which the soul has rejoined the universe as a whole. Hence KRSHNA's statement that the man may fall into a pit that is less deep, i.e., have better karma in the next life. Which doesn't give much comfort in this life.

** Buddhism teaches that while going through the karmic cycles, one may achieve a form of happiness in this life by disengaging from the issues that face one. While this does make life less stressful, it does nothing to resolve the immediate issue, which, in this case is the problem of sin.

*** MOSES lowers bread and wine. This is to recall the gift of Melchizedek at the spoils of the five kings. There, the King of Salem (peace) offers Abraham bread and wine. We are told by many scholars that Melchizedek is a symbol of Christ, to come, and in the seventh and tenth chapters of Hebrews, the writer draws a strong parallel between Jesus and Melchizedek. Thus when Moses teaches us in Genesis (and the rest of the Torah) to cover our sins by sacrifices, he is nonetheless pointing us to a more permanent solution to sin, namely, Jesus. Hence Moses sustains the man – for the teachings of the Tanakh are still of great value to us – but runs to find Jesus.

To further expand that theme: In Galatians 3:24, Paul tells us that the Law of Moses was our schoolmaster, or our tutor, to bring us to Jesus, in whom the Law is fulfilled. Thus Moses points to Jesus.

Appendix B
An Outline of the Bible

I. Garden:
   A. God created everything from nothing.
   B. God created Man and Woman.
   C. Mankind sinned against God.
   D. God began the long process of redemption.

II. Flood:
   A. Mankind became so evil that God decided to destroy them all and start over.
   B. Noah tried to follow God, so God chose to rescue him and his family.
   C. Noah built an ark on God's instruction, and rescued two of each animal.

III. Abraham:
   A. God spoke to Abraham, a man in Mesopotamia, and sent him across the desert with his clan.
   B. When Abraham reached modern day Israel, God promised it to Abraham's descendents.
   C. Abraham had a son, Isaac.
   D. Isaac had two sons, Esau and Jacob.
   E. Jacob had twelve sons by four wives.
   F. Jacob's favorite son, Joseph, the older son of his favorite wife, was hated by the other brothers. They faked his death and sold him into slavery.
   G. Joseph worked his way up, and with God's help became the third highest-ranking person in Egypt, responsible for storage and distribution of grain.
   H. Jacob and his family endured famine in Canaan. Jacob sent his sons to Egypt to buy grain.
   I. Joseph was reconciled with his brothers, and called them all down into Egypt, where they lived in the Nile delta (Goshen).

IV. Exodus and Journey to Canaan:
   A. There arose a Pharaoh who did not remember Joseph. He enslaved the Hebrews, and ordered that male Hebrew babies be killed at birth.

B. Moses was born a Hebrew. When his parents could hide him no longer, they put him in a basket of reeds and set him adrift on the Nile. He was found and raised by Pharaoh's sister.

C. Moses became aware of his Hebrew heritage. One day, on seeing a Hebrew beaten by an Egyptian, he killed the Egyptian.

D. Moses hid from justice in the barren deserts. There he married and became a shepherd.

E. One day, while watching flocks, Moses discovered a bush, on fire but not burned up. As he approached it, God spoke to him. God instructed Moses to return to Egypt and to free the Hebrew slaves, leading them to Canaan (Modern Israel).

F. Pharaoh was not willing to release the Hebrews, so God used ten plagues to persuade him. When Pharaoh changed his mind and chased Moses, God opened the Red Sea for their escape, then closed it onto the Egyptians.

G. Moses led the people first to the place where he had seen the burning bush. There, he received the Ten Commandments, which he showed to the people.

H. The Israelites began a long trip to the Promised Land. The tent of God's presence (the tabernacle, or place of worship) was always in the center of the camp. God was with them, "pitching His tent" among them.

I. After a long trip with many adventures, The Israelites reached the border of Canaan. They sent twelve spies. Ten spies gave a pessimistic report. Two gave a positive report.

J. Because they refused to go, Israel wandered in the desert for forty years, until a new generation, willing to go, arose.

K. Moses died, and Joshua took leadership of the nation.

V. Conquest and Judges:

A. Israel began to conquer Canaan, under Joshua's leadership. They subdued most of the land, but did not completely wipe out the prior residents.

B. After Joshua died, a pattern of behavior began:
   1. Israel would begin to fall away from God and worship idols.
   2. God would bring judgment or oppression upon them.
   3. The people would repent.
   4, God would bring a Judge, who would free them.
   5. When the Judge died, the cycle would repeat.

C. The last Judge, Samuel, appointed the first King, Saul.

VI. United Kingdom:
A. Saul reigned, but did evil before God. God shunned him and had Samuel anoint David, a shepherd boy, to be the next king.

B. Saul tried to have David killed, but eventually died.

C. David became King. He was a great general and a wise leader. This is considered Israel's Golden Age.

D. David sinned and tried to cover it up with murder. God judged the nation and David's family as a result. David repented.

E. After David's death, Solomon became king. He began as a wise king, but fell into idolatry as a result of political marriages.

F. Solomon built Solomon's Temple, the first of three temples to the Hebrew God.

VII. Divided Kingdom:
A. Following Solomon's death, the ten northern tribes broke away from the two southern tribes. The North was called Israel, and the South, Judah.

B. The kings of Israel and of Judah led the people through cycles similar to the pattern of the Judges. Slowly, the kings became more and more corrupt.

C. In time, God permitted Israel to be conquered by the Assyrian Empire. This was the Assyrian Captivity.

D. The ten northern tribes intermarried with the Assyrians, and lost their identity as a people. The New Testament Samaritans were descendents of these mixed marriages.

E. Babylon conquered Assyria.

F. In time, God permitted Judah to be conquered by the Babylonian Empire, ruled by Nebuchadnezzar. This was the Babylonian Captivity. Jews did not intermarry with Babylonians, and kept their cultural identity.

G. Later, some of the Jews were allowed to return and rebuild Jerusalem. This was when the second of the three temples was built.

H. Eventually the Jews were all allowed to return from Babylon.

VIII. Jesus' Ministry
A. 483 years after the second temple was built, Jesus was born to a virgin from the tribe of Judah.

B. When He was about 30 years old, He began to work miracles and to preach that the Messiah (the savior) had come.

C. Jesus claimed to be the messiah and the only Son of God.

D. When He was about 33 years old, Jesus was executed on false charges of blasphemy and of insurrection against Rome.

E. Jesus died for the sins of all mankind, and was buried.

F. Jesus rose again on the third day.

G. Jesus was seen by many, including his surviving disciples (Judas had hanged himself).

H. Jesus ascended bodily into heaven.

IX. Church Age

A. Fifty days after Jesus was killed, the assembled disciples and believers were filled with the Holy Spirit and began to preach. 3000 Jews were converted that day.

B. The church began to grow, and underwent persecution by the Jewish leaders.

C. The first deacon, Stephen, was martyred after preaching to the Pharisees.

D. Saul converted to Christianity after being blinded on the road to Damascus.

E. Peter saw a vision that instructed him to preach to Gentiles. He went with Cornelius to Antioch. A religious awakening began.

F. The church at Jerusalem sent Barnabas to find out what was happening at Antioch. He took Saul, who was now called Paul.

G. As a result of the gospel spreading to the gentiles at Antioch, Paul and Barnabas began a series of missionary journeys to Turkey, Greece, and Eastern Europe.

H. Paul was arrested because of a disturbance at Jerusalem. As a Roman Citizen, he appealed unto Caesar. He was taken to Rome. Along the route, Paul continued to spread the gospel.

I. Paul wrote a series of letters to various churches about religious matters. These letters form the majority of the New Testament.

J. The Apostle John was exiled at Patmos. There he saw a vision of the end times.

X. Future Events:

A. At an unknown date in the future, Jesus Christ will return suddenly and unexpectedly to reclaim His bride, which is the Church.

Appendix C
A Quick Survey of the Books of the Bible:

1. The TANAKH ("OLD TESTAMENT")

1.A. The TORAH
(The five books of the Law, also called the Books of Moses)

GENESIS: The book of the Beginning. This book covers the creation of everything, the first humans, the sin that separated humans from God, and the destruction of the world by the great flood. Many generations later, it tells of Abraham, a man God chose to start the long plan to rescue humans from the consequences of our sins. Abraham's great-grandson, through Godly wisdom and God's blessings, saves Egypt from a great famine.

EXODUS: The book of Going Out. This book begins 430 years after Genesis ends, when the people of Egypt have forgotten Joseph, and have begun to fear Joseph's people. God raises a leader named Moses to bring Abraham's descendents out of slavery in Egypt. God reveals the Ten Commandments, and sets the new nation, Israel, on a path to the land that God promised to Abraham.

LEVITICUS: The book of the Levites. This book gives greater detail concerning the commands given by God regarding every aspect of Israel's life.

NUMBERS: In this book, Israel's travels, and the events of their forty-year journey, are given in greater detail.

DEUTERONOMY: The book of the Second Law-giving. As he reaches the end of his life, Moses teaches the people one last time, telling the new generation all the things that God revealed to the previous generation.

1.B. The Writings:
(12 books of history, followed by 5 books of poetry)

JOSHUA: After the death of Moses, Joshua the son of Nun takes command of the people of Israel, and leads them into the Promised

Land. The book of Joshua details the conquest of Canaan (modern-day Israel).

JUDGES: After the death of Joshua, the people of Israel fell into a cycle of sin, judgment, repentance, and the rise of a Judge who freed them from foreign powers and led them back to God. This cycle repeats throughout Judges, and culminates in the rise of the last Judge, Samuel the High Priest.

RUTH: This simple love story, in which a foreign widow comes to Israel to take care of her also-widowed mother-in-law, is really about much more. The story of Boaz, the wealthy farmer who protects her and eventually marries her, is really the story of how Jesus sacrificially loves Israel.

1st & 2nd SAMUEL: The life and times of the last Judge of Israel, who appointed the first king of Israel, Saul. Saul fails to live up to his role as spiritual protector of Israel, and David, the great-grandson of Boaz and Ruth, is appointed to replace him.

1st & 2nd KINGS: The stories of the Kings of Israel, and later of Israel and Judah, from David until the Babylonian Captivity. Israel rebels against David's grandson, causing ten tribes to separate from the other two landed tribes. The ten are called Israel, and the two (Judah and Benjamin) are called Judah. *

1st & 2nd CHRONICLES: These books parallel the books of KINGS, detailing the slow decline of the nation as kings, some good and some evil, lead Israel and Judah first to follow God, and then to reject Him. The prophets (1.C.) mostly lived and wrote during this historical period. The CHRONICLES end after the ten tribes are overthrown by Assyria (The Assyrian Captivity) and then Assyria and the last two tribes are overthrown by Babylon (the Babylonian Captivity).

EZRA: After Babylon is overthrown by the Medio-Persian empire, a priest named Ezra leads some of the people of Israel back to Jerusalem, and attempts to rebuild the city. He is joined in this effort by Nehemiah.

NEHEMIAH: Nehemiah, a Jewish steward to Artaxerxes, is given special permission to return to Jerusalem and to rebuild it. This book describes his work there. Following this period, there is a gap in the canon until the time of Christ.

ESTHER: While Ezra and Nehemiah were rebuilding Jerusalem, a Jewish girl named Esther, back in the imperial capital, was chosen to be Artaxerxes' queen. She risked her life to uncover a plot against the Jews, and prevented the emperor from ordering all Jews in the empire to be killed. The last book of History.

JOB: The first book of poetry. Job loses everything but still praises God. How can we praise God when our lives fall apart around us? Job tells us. Also note chapter 19: "I know that my Redeemer lives…"

PSALMS: The songbook if Israel. Some were written by Moses, others by Asaph, and many by David. Note Psalm 22, a first-person description of crucifixion, written 500 years before crucifixion was invented. Note Psalm 23, also Psalm 139.

PROVERBS: A collection of wise sayings, composed and edited by Solomon, the son of David who succeeded him to the throne.

ECCLESIASTES: A book of wisdom in poetry that explores the meaning of life. It discusses how we ought to live in light of our own mortality, and of the non-permanent nature of physical things.

SONG of SOLOMON: Also called Song of Songs, Canticle of Canticles. A story of the love of a man for a woman and of a woman for a man.

1.C. The Prophets
5 major (longer) prophets, and 12 minor (shorter) prophets

ISAIAH: Isaiah wrote 66 chapter of prophecy during the period of the divided kingdom (before the Assyrian Captivity). Some historians believe that the work was written by as many as three men named Isaiah. This book begins with a call to repentance (see Is. 1:18) and warns Israel and Judah to repent while there is still time. It also hints very strongly of the coming of Jesus (See chapter 53, also chapter 9).

JEREMIAH: Jeremiah was called by God to preach to the last kings, even though his message was destined to be ignored. His book contains many important lessons for us today.

LAMENTATIONS: A second book by Jeremiah, in which he weeps about the judgment that is going to come upon Israel and Judah, first from the Assyrian invasion, and then from Babylon.

EZEKIEL: Ezekiel also preached to the last kings, and his prophecies are both among the strangest and the most uplifting of the Major Prophets.

DANIEL: Daniel begins by telling us about four young men (possibly teens) who were captured in the fall of Jerusalem and carried away to Babylon, where they were servants to Nebuchadnezzar and his successors. Daniel interpreted dreams, including Nebuchadnezzar's dream of the statue **. His three companions survived being burned alive, and Daniel survived being thrown into a lion's den during the Medio-Persians conquered Babylon. Daniel went on to record many prophecies, including the prediction of Jesus' birth after 483 years (69 weeks of years "until Shiloh comes").

The Minor Prophets:

HOSEA: In the time of the last kings, Hosea compares God to the husband of an unfaithful wife.

JOEL: In this book, God promises to pour out His Spirit upon mankind in the last days.

AMOS: Warns of the coming Assyrian and Babylonian captivity, when both Israel and Judah will be conquered and destroyed. But a few will be allowed to return.

OBADIAH: The judgment that will fall on Israel will not spare the neighboring nations.

JONAH: We all know the fish story, but we sometimes miss the clear picture of God's mercy on the people of Ninevah (one-time capital of Assyria), despite the prophet's reluctant message.

MICAH: God predicts the exact city in which the Messiah will be born (Bethlehem). With Daniel's 483 years, this gives us a pretty exact time and place… Also note 6:8. "He has told you, O Man, what is good, and what the Lord requires of thee…"

NAHUM: Warning that the spiritual watchmen of Israel, the shepherds who should be leading them to God, have fallen asleep.

HABAKKUK: Judgment is coming because Israel is engaged in idol worship. Habakkuk mocks those who build a stone idol and then pretend that it is alive and can save them.

ZEPHANIAH: Begs Israel and Judah to return to God, so that they will not face the coming invasions. Remarks on God's love for Israel and Judah, and His reluctance to let them go. Reveals God's promise to restore them.

HAGGAI: During the Babylonian captivity, when the Medio-Persian kings were sending people back to Israel and Judah, Haggai warns them not to return to the old ways of sin and idolatry. He reminds them that God has chosen them, and has begun the promised restoration.

ZECHARIAH: In the time when Nehemiah is rebuilding the temple, God announces that the Messiah will be betrayed for 30 silver coins, and that the coins will buy a field for the burial of strangers. Compare the story of Judas in the New Testament. Also note chapter 3, the trial of Joshua the High Priest, who, though clearly guilty, is held blameless.

MALACHI: Last book of the Tanakh ("Old Testament"). Predicts that a prophet (John the Baptist) will go before the Messiah, to clear His path and prepare people for His coming. Reproves the people during the restoration of Israel, reminding them to be holy and to serve no idols.

---

* There is a thirteenth tribe, Levi, but it had no land, and usually is not counted among the "twelve" tribes (or "the landed tribes").

** The dream involved a statue with a golden head symbolizing Babylon, a silver chest and arms symbolizing the Medio-Persian Empire, a bronze abdomen and thighs, representing the Greek Empire of Alexander, and finally iron legs and feet, representing Rome. The feet and toes were mixed with clay, representing the fragility and corruption of the Roman Empire. From this, we obtain the expression, "Feet of clay" to refer to a person who has unseen faults which undermine his integrity.

During the time of the iron feet, a block of stone is cut from a mountain by a spiritual force, and is thrown against the statue, shattering it. This represents the rise of Jesus and Christianity during the Roman period.

Daniel also gave us several detailed prophecies concerning the historical period between the fall of the Babylonian Empire and the rise of Rome. Comparisons of these with secular history can be quite interesting.

2. The New Testament

MATTHEW: A biography of Jesus, with an eye towards the fulfillment of prophecies. Written by Jesus' follower, Matthew, also called Levi, Son of Alphaeus.

MARK: A biography of Jesus. The shortest of the biographies, but also the oldest. Written by John Mark, a follower of Paul, Peter, and Barnabas, based largely on the recollections of Peter (also called Simon, son of Jonah).

LUKE: The longest and most detailed biography of Jesus, based on collected accounts gathered and arranged by Luke, a physician who followed Paul on his missionary journeys. Luke also wrote The Acts of the Apostles.

JOHN: A biography of Jesus told as a series of short scenes, with less attention to chronology and more descriptions of speeches by Jesus. Written by John, one of Jesus' followers, and by some accounts His best friend.

THE ACTS OF THE APOSTLES: Also called Acts. The birth of the early church, and its life. Jesus orders his disciples to spread the gospel through the entire world, then returns to heaven. God reveals to Peter that Gentiles can become Christians. The early church goes through crisis and persecution, but only becomes stronger. An enemy of the church, Saul of Tarsus, becomes a Christian and takes on the name Paul. Under the guidance of Barnabas, Paul begins to share the gospel in Asia Minor and in Greece. Eventually Paul is arrested for causing riots, but the gospel continues to spread across Europe. Acts was written by Luke, an associate of Paul.

ROMANS: A letter by Paul to a church that he started in Rome. In this letter, Paul explains the relationships between sin, death, the law, salvation, and life. From this book, the "Roman Road" to salvation is drawn. We all sin, sin kills us, God loves us, God offers us life through the sacrifice of Jesus, and we can be saved from the consequences of our sins if we trust in Jesus.

1st CORINTHIANS: Paul writes to a church that he started in Greece, explaining how to live like Christians. In places he encourages them, and in other places he lovingly rebukes them. Paul explains the Lord's supper, spiritual gifts, what to do about meat that has been sacrificed to idols, * and the true meaning of love. Note especially chapter 13, the love chapter, in which Paul explains Christian love, and states that without love, all other Christian practices are pointless.

2nd CORINTHIANS: The folks at Corinth didn't pay attention to the first letter, and needed a reminder. Paul rebukes them for listening to false teachers, and reminds them of the importance of following Jesus, not an earthly leader. Paul points out that we are like clay pots (i.e., composed of the same elements as dirt) and yet, hidden within us is the treasure of God's glory and God's Spirit. He describes how, even though we suffer persecution for being Christians, we will never be completely crushed. Paul explains that those who believe in Christ are new creatures, and that their old lives have passed away.

GALATIANS: Paul writes to a church that he started in Galatia, in an area we would now call Turkey. Paul rebukes them for listening to false teachers, who tried to confuse them with complicated religious rules and superstitions. He reminds them of the gospel he taught them, and says that if even an angel from heaven were to come and try to teach a different religious teaching, they should ignore it. He points out to them that whatever they sow they will reap, and then encourages them not to grow tired of doing good, because in time God will bless their work.

EPHESIANS: Paul writes to a church that he started in Greece, and points out that they were not saved because of anything they had done, but because of their faith in God, which itself came from God. Paul reminds them of the sacrifice of Christ for their sins, and explains how to live as Christians, with an emphasis on loving their families. Paul tells us that the Christian fight is not against human evil, but against spiritual powers. He tells us to arm ourselves against trials and temptations.

PHILIPPIANS: Paul writes to the church at Philippi, in Greece. He tells them how they make his heart rejoice when he thinks of them, and of the good works that they have done in Christ. He is especially encouraged by their generosity to him, and to fellow Christians who have suffered hardships and trials. He rejoices in their love, and encourages them to rejoice in the Lord always. He tells them that even though he is on trial for his life, he cannot lose: If he lives, he lives for Christ; if he dies, he goes to the presence of Christ. Paul encourages the Philippians to be humble, as Jesus who was God Incarnate made Himself humble. Paul reminds them of Jesus washing the feet of His disciples, and finally allowing Himself to be shamefully tortured and executed for the sins of the humans that He Himself had made. Paul finishes the letter with an order to rejoice.

COLOSSIANS: Paul writes to the church he founded in Colossae, and discusses the nature of Jesus and of His incarnation. He reminds them not to be bound by pagan superstitions. He encourages them to instead set their eyes on things eternal, and explains once more how to live as Christians in a pagan world.

1st & 2nd THESSALONIANS: Paul writes two letters to the church that he founded in Thessaloniki. In the first letter, he talks about his travels with his disciple, Timothy. Then he discusses the return of Jesus at the end of time. Finally, he instructs them on how to live as Christians, constantly in prayer, and rejoicing in good works. In the second letter, he encourages them and warns them against false teachers.

1st & 2nd TIMOTHY: Paul writes two letters to his disciple, Timothy, whom Paul trained to be a church planter and a leader like himself. In these books, Paul talks about how to lead a church, and how the church should conduct itself. He also describes the importance of the scripture, which he says is the breath of God.

TITUS: Paul writes to another of his disciples, Titus, and gives him guidance about the church Titus is founding on Crete.

PHILEMON: Paul, in Rome, has encountered and converted a runaway slave named Onesimus. Paul happens to know Onesimus' former master, a man named Philemon, so Paul sends Onesimus back to him with this letter. In it, Paul offers to pay any damages caused by Onesimus, and strongly encourages Philemon to treat him not as a slave, but as a brother in Christ. This was a radical teaching in 1st century Rome: That even the lowest slave is our brother, and worthy of our respect.

HEBREWS: The authorship of Hebrews is uncertain, but the writer knew Paul and Timothy, and was an associate of other apostles. Paul and Barnabas are the two leading contenders for possible authors. The book strongly encourages all Christians, and especially those of a Hebrew heritage. It speaks about the fulfillment of God's plan through Jesus. It is a powerful book of encouragement.

The writer speaks in chapter 7 of Jesus as the once-forever high priest prophesied in Psalms 110:3. He explains that while human priests must offer sacrifice for their own sin before offering sacrifice for ours, Jesus, being sinless, could approach the altar directly. In chapter 10, we see Jesus, the High Priest, carrying Jesus, the Sacrifice, to the altar of Jesus, Almighty God. Jesus did it all, and there is nothing left for us to do but to love Him and to accept what He has done for us.

Chapter 11 discusses faith, first defining it, and then explaining how it is vital if we wish to please God. He then gives examples from the Tanakh (Old Testament) of heroes who lived by faith. Even though these were flawed and sinful people, their lives were dominated by faith. In Genesis we read that Abraham believed God, and it was counted to him as righteousness. The roll call of the faithful, in chapter 11, also consists of people made righteous by faith. Hebrews concludes with instructions for how to live by faith.

JAMES: This letter was written by James, the brother of Jesus.** In this short but pointed letter, James gives clear instructions to the church, and reminds us to pray. He calls for equal treatment of the rich and the poor, and reminds us of the need for practical action. He points out that a true faith will be demonstrated in good deeds, and that while good deeds do not save us from sin, they do grow naturally from our Christian lifestyle. James talks about the danger of the human tongue, and encourages believers to flee from evil. He concludes by pointing out that the fervent prayer of a righteous man does much good.

1st & 2nd PETER: Peter writes to all the churches, reminding them to follow the teachings Jesus set out, and to leave their old ways behind. He warns of false teachers who will lead them astray, and encourages them to stay close to God.

1st JOHN: John, author of John's gospel, writes to the churches and encourages them to love one another. He warns them that those who deny that they sin make a liar of God, but that those who confess their sins will be forgiven, as God is faithful and just. He encourages believers to turn from their former lives and to leave sin behind them. He reminds us of the great love that God ahs for us, and tells us to love one another.

2nd JOHN: John writes to a specific church and cautions them about well-known sin in their midst. He warns of false teachers, and calls for them to avoid such men.

3rd JOHN: John rejoices in the good report he has heard concerning this particular church. He calls out one person for bad behavior, and cautions others not to be like him. Then he commends a brother who is known for good works.

JUDE: Jude, an early disciple, writes a letter to all Christians. In it, he warns them about false teachers, and reminds them of the judgment that fell on false teachers in the Tanakh (Old Testament). He warns them to avoid mockers of the gospel, and encourages them to be ready for Jesus to return.

REVELATION: In this book, the Apostle John, author of four other New Testament books, records a vision that he saw while he was in exile on an island for preaching the gospel. First, he sees a vision of Jesus Christ, who gives him messages for the seven churches.*** Then he is taken to heaven, where he sees the events leading to the end of the world. Finally, he is shown a new heaven and a new earth, ruled by Jesus Himself.

* The folks are Corinth were surrounded by pagan temples, and sometimes could buy meat cheaply because it had been on an altar at a temple somewhere. Some folks reasoned that it was perfectly good meat, since the idols weren't real. Others did not want to condone the worship of idols in any way, and considered the meat tainted. Paul affirms that the meat is perfectly good to eat, but introduces a principle of Christian behavior: If eating meat would make a weaker brother stumble in his faith, then Paul would never eat meat again. Our behavior needs to be based on love for other brothers and sisters in Christ.

** Some denominations interpret brother to mean a male relative, especially a cousin or a relative of similar age. Other denominations take this to mean a half-brother of Jesus, i.e., a natural son of Mary and Joseph. In either case, this would be a close relative who did not believe during Jesus' lifetime, but came to believe after His resurrection from the dead.

*** There are various interpretation of the meanings of the seven churches. Some see it as types of churches that have existed at all times. That is, there has always been a church that placed too much emphasis on doctrine, and not enough on love, as at Ephesus. Or that there was always a church that had a name for being alive, but was dead, as at Sardis. Others have seen this as seven stages in the progress of the church, from the time of the apostles until now. Still others see this as seven models of the human heart, or states into which a Christian may fall.

In any case, we should avoid the errors of the five churches that are reprimanded:
1. Ephesus, reprimanded for concentrating on sound doctrine and forgetting to love God and each other;
2. Pergamum, reprimanded for putting up with false teachers who taught people to sin;
3. Thyatira, reprimanded for having a false prophetess who led people into idolatry;

4. Sardis, reprimanded for having a name that it is alive, but being dead – that is, showing no signs of life, and not fulfilling its purpose as a church of the Living God.
5. Laodicea, reprimanded for being neither hot nor cold, but lukewarm; that is, not being pagan, and able to be converted; but not being fully committed to Christ, and doing the duties of a church.

Two churches are not reprimanded:
1. Smyrna, which is under persecution but remains faithful, and
2. Philadelphia, which has kept the word of God, and not denied His Name.

It is safe to say that there are churches like each of these examples in our world today. Let us learn hence not to endure false teachers, as did Pergamum and Thyatira; at the other extreme not to be so committed to doctrine that we forget to love God and other humans, as did Ephesus.

Let us remain alive in God, and not allow our hearts to grow cold, as did Sardis. Let us retain our passion for God, and not grow lukewarm, as did Laodicea. Instead, let us remain faithful, like Smyrna, and keep God's Word, like Philadelphia.

Appendix D:
Creeds and Statements of Faith:

The Pre-Pauline Doctrine:
From 1 Corinthians 15:3-8, 24-26 (KJV)

3 For I delivered unto you first of all that which I also received, how that Christ died for our sins according to the scriptures;
4 And that he was buried, and that he rose again the third day according to the scriptures:
5 And that he was seen of Cephas, then of the twelve:
6 After that, he was seen of above five hundred brethren at once; of whom the greater part remain unto this present, but some are fallen asleep.
7 After that, he was seen of James; then of all the apostles.
8 And last of all he was seen of me also, as of one born out of due time. ...
24 Then cometh the end, when he shall have delivered up the kingdom to God, even the Father; when he shall have put down all rule and all authority and power.
25 For he must reign, till he hath put all enemies under his feet.
26 The last enemy that shall be destroyed is death.

This is the oldest statement of faith and doctrine found in all of Christianity. Paul is quoting directly from teachings he learned from the other apostles, after his Damascus Road conversion. Even the most skeptical of scholars place the composition of this doctrine within months after the crucifixion, and some place it within weeks or days of the crucifixion.

It is also noteworthy that the phrase "according to the scriptures" occurs repeatedly. Since the gospels were not yet written, Paul is clearly speaking of the Tanakh or Old Testament, and passages such as Isaiah 53 (cited in Acts 8:32-33 when Philip explained the gospel to the Ethiopian eunuch) or Psalm 22, among many others.

The Pre-Pauline Doctrine (so called because it originated before Paul was converted to Christianity) has five main points: That Jesus died for the sins of mankind, and was buried, rose again, and was seen by many (vv.3-8), and shall return on the last day (vv. 24-26). Please read the entire chapter.

It cannot be emphasized too strongly that a creed, or any tradition composed by men, is merely an attempt to better understand what the Bible teaches. The first and best source for doctrine is the Bible, above all else. If you should discover that any phrase, word, or comma in any creed can not be supported by the Bible itself, you are urged to lay that creed aside, and to draw doctrine fresh from the source, which is the Word of God.

The Apostles' Creed:

1. I believe in God the Father, Almighty, Maker of heaven and earth:

2. And in Jesus Christ, his only begotten Son, our Lord:

3. Who was conceived by the Holy Ghost, born of the Virgin Mary:

4. Suffered under Pontius Pilate; was crucified, dead and buried: He descended into hell:

5. The third day he rose again from the dead:

6. He ascended into heaven, and sits at the right hand of God the Father Almighty:

7. From thence he shall come to judge the quick and the dead:

8. I believe in the Holy Ghost:

9. I believe in the holy catholic church: the communion of saints:

10. The forgiveness of sins:

11. The resurrection of the body:

12. And the life everlasting. Amen.

This is a simple early creed with which nearly all Christians can agree. Note that "catholic" means "all-encompassing."

The Nicene Creed

I believe in one God, the Father Almighty, Maker of heaven and earth, and of all things visible and invisible.

And in one Lord Jesus Christ, the only-begotten Son of God, begotten of the Father before all worlds; God of God, Light of Light, very God of very God; begotten, not made, being of one substance with the Father, by whom all things were made.

Who, for us men for our salvation, came down from heaven, and was incarnate by the Holy Spirit of the virgin Mary, and was made man; and was crucified also for us under Pontius Pilate; He suffered and was buried; and the third day He rose again, according to the Scriptures; and ascended into heaven, and sits on the right hand of the Father; and He shall come again, with glory, to judge the quick and the dead; whose kingdom shall have no end.

And I believe in the Holy Ghost, the Lord and Giver of Life; who proceeds from the Father [and the Son]; who with the Father and the Son together is worshipped and glorified; who spoke by the prophets.

And I believe one holy catholic and apostolic Church. I acknowledge one baptism for the remission of sins; and I look for the resurrection of the dead, and the life of the world to come. Amen.

The key difference between this creed and the Apostles' Creed is that the Nicene more clearly explains the roles and the nature of the Trinity. .
There are other creeds, such as the Athanasian Creed, which spells out the nature of the Trinity and of Christ even more clearly, but the three statements of faith above should suffice as a simple explanation of what Christians believe.

Appendix E:
The Romans Road
"What must I do to be saved?"

The oldest question on Christianity is "What must I do to be saved?" In order to give a clear and concise but Bible-based answer to this question, the "Romans Road" has been composed. Some versions of it start with chapter 1, and draw a verse from each chapter through chapter 10. For our purposes, however, four verses will be sufficient.

Romans 3:23
For all have sinned and fallen short of the glory of God.

Romans 6:23
For the wages of sin is death, but the gift of God is eternal Life through Jesus Christ, Our Lord.

Romans 5:8
But God demonstrates His love towards us, in that while we were still sinners, Christ died for us.

Romans 10:9
If you confess with your mouth Jesus as Lord, and believe in your heart that God has raised Him from the dead, you shall be saved.

Those simple verses are show a simple Biblical explanation for how to be saved: Understanding that you are a sinner, and doomed to be apart from God forever, but that God loves you despite your sin, you must confess that Jesus is Lord, and believe that God raised Him from the dead. Many people do this in the form of a prayer, but it is not a question of saying the "magic words" or of following a certain "magic formula."

The common element in Biblical examples of salvation is belief in Jesus' death, burial, and resurrection. If you need a formula to follow, Romans 10:9 is a great place to begin, and as Paul tells us just moments later, "Whosoever calls upon the name of the Lord shall be saved."

In the scripture, there are many examples of people becoming Christians. Let's examine a few:

Luke 23:39-43 NASB

39 One of the criminals who were hanged [there] was hurling abuse at Him, saying, "Are You not the Christ? Save Yourself and us!"

40 But the other answered, and rebuking him said, "Do you not even fear God, since you are under the same sentence of condemnation?

41 "And we indeed [are suffering] justly, for we are receiving what we deserve for our deeds; but this man has done nothing wrong."

42 And he was saying, "Jesus, remember me when You come in Your kingdom!"

43 And He said to him, "Truly I say to you, today you shall be with Me in Paradise."

Acts 2:37-38

37 Now when they heard this, they were pricked in their heart, and said unto Peter and to the rest of the apostles, Men and brethren, what shall we do?

38 Then Peter said unto them, Repent, and be baptized every one of you in the name of Jesus Christ for the remission of sins, and ye shall receive the gift of the Holy Ghost.

Acts 8:35-36

35 Then Philip opened his mouth, and began at the same scripture, and preached unto him Jesus.

36 And as they went on their way, they came unto a certain water: and the eunuch said, See, here is water; what doth hinder me to be baptized?

Act 9:17-18

17 And Ananias went his way, and entered into the house; and putting his hands on him said, Brother Saul, the Lord, Jesus, that appeared unto thee in the way as thou camest, hath sent me, that thou mightest receive thy sight, and be filled with the Holy Ghost.

18 *And immediately there fell from his eyes as it had been scales: and he received sight forthwith, and arose, and was baptized.*

Acts 10:44-48
44 While Peter yet spake these words, the Holy Ghost fell on all them which heard the word.

45 And they of the circumcision which believed were astonished, as many as came with Peter, because that on the Gentiles also was poured out the gift of the Holy Ghost.

46 For they heard them speak with tongues, and magnify God. Then answered Peter,

47 Can any man forbid water, that these should not be baptized, which have received the Holy Ghost as well as we?

48 And he commanded them to be baptized in the name of the Lord. Then prayed they him to tarry certain days.

Acts 13:12
Then the deputy, when he saw what was done, believed, being astonished at the doctrine of the Lord

Acts 13:48
And when the Gentiles heard this, they were glad, and glorified the word of the Lord: and as many as were ordained to eternal life believed.

Acts16:30-31
30 And brought them out, and said, Sirs, what must I do to be saved?

31 And they said, Believe on the Lord Jesus Christ, and thou shalt be saved, and thy house.

Acts 17:11-12

11 These were more noble than those in Thessalonica, in that they received the word with all readiness of mind, and searched the scriptures daily, whether those things were so.

12 Therefore many of them believed; also of honourable women which were Greeks, and of men, not a few.

Acts 18:8
And Crispus, the chief ruler of the synagogue, believed on the Lord with all his house; and many of the Corinthians hearing believed, and were baptized.

Acts 19:4-5
4 Then said Paul, John verily baptized with the baptism of repentance, saying unto the people, that they should believe on him which should come after him, that is, on Christ Jesus.

5 When they heard this, they were baptized in the name of the Lord Jesus.

These are examples from the book of Acts, and it would do us good to examine each and to draw general common principles from them. In nearly every case, the gospel was shared with the people just before they believed, and in each case they believed the gospel, and specifically believed on the Lord Jesus Christ.

There are a few instances in the gospels themselves that seem to shed light on this question as well, so we should include them in our study. Some people reasonably ask if these can be called salvation events, since the resurrection in which they were to believe had not yet occurred. Perhaps they were merely preparation for that resurrection. Still, it behooves us to examine them.

Matt. 16:15-16
15 He saith unto them, But whom say ye that I am?

16 And Simon Peter answered and said, Thou art the Christ, the Son of the living God.

John 11:23-27

24 Martha saith unto him, I know that he shall rise again in the resurrection at the last day.

25 Jesus said unto her, I am the resurrection, and the life: he that believeth in me, though he were dead, yet shall he live:

26 And whosoever liveth and believeth in me shall never die. Believest thou this?

27 She saith unto him, Yea, Lord: I believe that thou art the Christ, the Son of God, which should come into the world.

John 20:27-29

27 Then saith he to Thomas, Reach hither thy finger, and behold my hands; and reach hither thy hand, and thrust it into my side: and be not faithless, but believing.

28 And Thomas answered and said unto him, My Lord and my God.

29 Jesus saith unto him, Thomas, because thou hast seen me, thou hast believed: blessed are they that have not seen, and yet have believed.

Recommended Reading

These are books that you might find helpful as you grow in the Christian faith. Remember that they must not replace the Bible, either as the focus of your time or the focus of your doctrine. The Bible is the only sure and certain guide to what we should believe. These books are intended to help you understand the Bible's truths, and if they fail in that, ignore these books.

It should also be said that Christian Growth is organic. If you spend time reading the Bible, pray regularly, and meet regularly with fellow believers, growth is inevitable. Just as a farmer does not actually cause the plant to grow, but simply provides an environment conducive to growth – the plant does all the work – so also you need to create an environment conducive to growth. Perhaps these books may make your heart and mind better suited to grow the seed that the Bible plants within you.

Mere Christianity, by C.S. Lewis.

Lewis presents the core of Christianity, that is, "Mere" Christianity, without all the incense, candles, other trappings. In the introduction, he presents the idea of Christianity as a large house with many rooms, representing the denominations. He urges believers to find the room best suited to them.

Throughout the book, Lewis argues for a simple yet logical understanding of the faith. Two significant arguments he presents are the poached egg argument and the argument from desire. Please take note of each.

Survival Kit for New Christians, by Ralph W. Neighbour

This simple but interesting study is designed to help new Christians become firmly planted in the gospel. It offers practical steps and introduces the basic doctrines of Christianity. Easy to follow instructions set the new believer on the right path.

Everlasting Man, The, by G.K. Chesterton.

Chesterton poses two arguments: That mankind is different from all other creatures, and that Jesus of Nazareth was different from all other humans. Chesterton specifically opposes the idea that humans are merely more intelligent animals. He remarks on the

Lascaux Cave paintings; that it is remarkable to have dug in the earth and found them, then asks how deep we should dig to find where an animal had painted an image of a human.

He also presents the roots of an argument that Lewis later develops as the poached egg argument.

Screwtape Letters, The, by C.S. Lewis

Lewis presents a work of fiction, based on the pretense of having intercepted letters exchanged between demons, concerning the best ways to damn humans. While darkly comical in one sense, this book is oddly accurate, even haunting, and the reader may find himself wondering how Lewis knew his inner thoughts. Lewis offers an unmatchable guide to understanding and overcoming temptations. We see a picture of God from the other perspective, and we are called to ponder the depth of God's glory and love.

Experiencing God, by Henry Blackaby, Jr.

Blackaby examines the moment when life events challenge a Christian and threaten his faith. He points to individuals in the Bible who met a challenge and who chose to trust God through a crisis of faith. By examining these case studies, we are able to see how we should respond when an event arises that seems to huge for us.

More Than a Carpenter, by Josh McDowell

McDowell presents a serious discussion on the Christian faith, and whether it is reasonable in the modern world. He offers several arguments, and uses C.S. Lewis' poached egg argument to create a three-horned dilemma (or trilemma, as he styles it). When faced with the known facts about Jesus of Nazareth, we really have only three options for what to believe, and two of them don't fit.

Who Moved the Stone? by Frank Morrison

Frank Morrison reviews the last week of Jesus' life with a critical eye, and tries to reconcile the known facts and the given accounts. He comes to a remarkable conclusion: That if the Jesus of Nazareth did not rise from the dead, then the Jewish authorities and the Roman rulers had an easy means to prove that He was still dead. And yet, they did not.

Morrison examines the various possibilities, and they finally culminate in a single unanswerable question: Who moved the stone?

Case for Christ, The, by Lee Stroebel

When Lee Stroebel's wife converted to Christianity, Lee Stroebel, a staunch atheist and a writer for the Chicago Tribune, set out to prove to her that Christianity was impossible. The religion editor offered an easy method to destroy Christianity: Prove that Jesus of Nazareth did not rise from the dead.

To Stroebel's dismay, and despite his best efforts to remain an atheist, his investigation began to lead him in the wrong direction, culminating in his own conversion.

Cold Case Christianity, by J. Warner Wallace

Like Lee Stroebel, J. Warner Wallace was happy as an atheist until his wife converted to Christianity. Determined to "debunk" her faith, he used his training as a homicide detective specializing in cold cases to critically examine the gospels. To his surprise, he quickly found them to be authentic witness statements, and his comparison of the testimonies led him to a shocking truth.

Wallace goes on to present the provenance of the statements as a chain of custody handed down through the generations to the present day.

Till We Have Faces, by C. S. Lewis and Helen J. Lewis

The Lewises retell the ancient myth of Eros and Psyche, from Greek mythology, but use it as an analogy to Christian truth. The protagonist lives a difficult life, rising in the end to respect and power. At the end of her life, she, like Job, seeks an audience with Deity in order to find justice – but the result is not what she had hoped to find.

My Confession, by Leo Count Tolstoy*

Leo Tolstoy, one of the greatest writers of all times, reflects on his spiritual journey, and remarks on how easily his very weak Christian faith was demolished in his youth. He presents other examples of faith too weak to stand against even a single question. Even though he saw himself as an intellectual and a leader in the thought of his day, and was successful as a writer and philosopher, Tolstoy found his life empty and meaningless.

He became obsessed with finding a reason to live, a purpose to his life, or any single goal that would make his life more than an ephemeral spark. In the end, he came to the conclusion that there is only one bridge between the finite and the infinite: The Christian faith. Only this faith makes sense of the lives we lead.

Orthodoxy, by G.K. Chesterton

Imagine an explorer with very poor navigation skills, who lands upon a distant beach and claims it in the name of God and King, only to find that it is a popular seafront resort in his own country. This is where Chesterton found himself, after attempting to create his own reasonable doctrinal system, then suddenly discovering that his new discovery was in fact what the church had been teaching for centuries.

God in the Dock, by C.S. Lewis

During World War II, Lewis gave a series of lectures over the radio, in the hopes of offering spiritual comfort to a hurting nation. This book is a compilation of those addresses, and offers answers to many hard questions about God and the Christian Faith.

Easter, Fact or Fiction, by Chase A. Thompson

Thompson offers 20 sound reasons to believe in the fact of the resurrection of Jesus Christ. The book is easy to read and yet very compelling. My personal favorite among the 20 reasons is the Lithuanian argument. Should you ever meet Chase, be sure to ask him which three nations border Lithuania. Spoiler alert: the capital of Lithuania is Vilnius.

---

*Leo Count Tolstoy, the Russian nobleman best known for his novel *War and Peace,* must not be confused with Leo Tolstoy, the Cossack, who wrote about his cavalry experiences burning villages in his book *Bright.*

Lightning Source UK Ltd.
Milton Keynes UK
UKHW011138030323
417986UK00001B/48